VAJRA SPEECH

RANGJUNG YESHE BOOKS · WWW.RANGJUNG.COM

PADMASAMBHAVA · *Treasures from Juniper Ridge* · *Advice from the Lotus-Born* · *Dakini Teachings* · *Following in Your Footsteps: The Lotus-Born Guru in Nepal*

PADMASAMBHAVA AND JAMGÖN KONGTRÜL · *The Light of Wisdom, Vol. 1, & Vol. 2, Vol. 3, Secret, Vol. 4 & Vol. 5*

PADMASAMBHAVA, CHOKGYUR LINGPA, JAMYANG KHYENTSE WANGPO, TULKU URGYEN RINPOCHE, ORGYEN TOBGYAL RINPOCHE, & OTHERS · *Dispeller of Obstacles* · *The Tara Compendium* · *Powerful Transformation* · *Dakini Activity*

YESHE TSOGYAL · *The Lotus-Born*

DAKPO TASHI NAMGYAL · *Clarifying the Natural State*

TSELE NATSOK RANGDRÖL · *Mirror of Mindfulness* · *Heart Lamp* · *Empowerment and Samaya*

CHOKGYUR LINGPA · *Ocean of Amrita* · *The Great Gate* · *Skillful Grace* · *Great Accomplishment* · *Guru Heart Practices*

TRAKTUNG DUDJOM LINGPA · *A Clear Mirror*

JAMGÖN MIPHAM RINPOCHE · *Gateway to Knowledge, Vol. 1, Vol. 2, Vol. 3, & Vol. 4*

TULKU URGYEN RINPOCHE · *Blazing Splendor* · *Rainbow Painting* · *As It Is, Vol. 1 & Vol. 2* · *Vajra Speech* · *Repeating the Words of the Buddha* · *Dzogchen Deity Practice* · *Vajra Heart Revisited*

ADEU RINPOCHE · *Freedom in Bondage*

KHENCHEN THRANGU RINPOCHE · *King of Samadhi* · *Crystal Clear*

CHÖKYI NYIMA RINPOCHE · *Present Fresh Wakefulness* · *Bardo Guidebook*

TULKU THONDUP · *Enlightened Living*

ORGYEN TOBGYAL RINPOCHE · *Life & Teachings of Chokgyur Lingpa* · *Straight Talk*

DZIGAR KONGTRÜL RINPOCHE · *Uncommon Happiness*

TSOKNYI RINPOCHE · *Fearless Simplicity* · *Carefree Dignity*

MARCIA BINDER SCHMIDT · *Dzogchen Primer* · *Dzogchen Essentials* · *Quintessential Dzogchen* · *Confessions of a Gypsy Yogini* · *Precious Songs of Awakening Compilation*

ERIK PEMA KUNSANG · *Wellsprings of the Great Perfection* · *A Tibetan Buddhist Companion* · *The Rangjung Yeshe Tibetan-English Dictionary of Buddhist Culture & Perfect Clarity*

VAJRA SPEECH

PITH INSTRUCTIONS
FOR THE DZOGCHEN YOGI

TULKU URGYEN RINPOCHE

Translated from the Tibetan by
Erik Pema Kunsang

Compiled by
Marcia Binder Schmidt
and edited with
Michael Tweed

RANGJUNG YESHE ✦ *Boudhanath, Hong Kong & Esby* ✦ 2001

RANGJUNG YESHE PUBLICATIONS
Flat 5a, Greenview Garden,
125 Robinson Road, Hong Kong
www.rangjung.com

ADDRESS LETTERS TO:

editor@rangjung.com
Rangjung Yeshe Publications
Ka-Nying Shedrub Ling Monastery
P.O. Box 1200, Kathmandu, Nepal

FIRST EDITION 2001

PUBLICATION DATA:
Tulku Urgyen Rinpoche (1920–1996).
Translated from the Tibetan
by Erik Pema Kunsang (Erik Hein Schmidt).
Compiled by Marcia Binder Schmidt
and edited with Michael Tweed.

FIRST ED.

Title: Vajra Speech
ISBN 978-962-7341-44-4 (pbk.)
1. Vajrayana — tradition of pith instructions.
2. Buddhism — Tibet. I. Title.

PREFACE

This book is an offering to practitioners who aspire to realize the meaning of the Great Perfection in actuality. We hope that you can turn to any page for inspiration and, additionally, use *Vajra Speech* to clear up your doubts.

Tulku Urgyen Rinpoche's approach was to teach the great views of Buddhist practice as one unified path. He brought the essential points of Prajnaparamita, the Middle Way, Mahamudra and Dzogchen together within the recognition of and training in the natural state of original mind. All the various practices with effort, he explained, share that single aim and are skillful means to not only remove the hindrances for realization but also to enhance our progress once we have glimpsed our intrinsic nature.

Please understand that the context of this practice advice is primarily that of effortless meditation, which necessitates having been introduced to that type of training. If you have not received such teachings, please do so. At the same time, please continue with whatever practice system in which you are already involved.

Tulku Urgyen Rinpoche in no way encouraged using the concept of effortlessness as an excuse for disregarding the need to purify our habitual tendencies and obscurations.

Orgyen Tobgyal Rinpoche has said about Tulku Urgyen Rinpoche, "I feel certain that there is not the slightest difference between the state of mind of Tulku Urgyen Rinpoche and Samantabhadra. Both Dzongsar Khyentse Rinpoche and myself felt that compared to many months and years of studying books and going through analytical meditation, it was more beneficial to spend just a few hours asking questions of Tulku Urgyen and listening to his answers."

Here, we offer some answers. May they benefit countless beings.

Erik & Marcia

Tulku Urgyen Rinpoche

Malaysia, early seventies

ACCOMPLISHMENT

སྒྲུབ་རྟགས།

Among the signs of practice, there is experience and accomplishment. The true sign of practice is that you are naturally and effortlessly without fixation. Also, that you are endowed with devotion, compassion and pure perception, just like the sky is filled with the warmth of sunlight.

∾

All accomplishment comes through recognizing the thatness of mind. Without recognizing this, whatever we do is upside down.

∾

To trust the consequence of karma is a true accomplishment of Dharma practice.

Another true accomplishment is to be unharmed by the experiences of bliss, clarity and nonthought, while being free from the two hindrances to meditation: drowsiness and agitation.

∾

Do not attach any importance to temporary experiences, none whatsoever. There is only one thing to be confident in, the true state of realization that is unchanging like space. Understanding this is of utmost importance. What really matters is to increase your devotion to and confidence in the Dharma, so that from within you feel that only the Dharma matters, that only practice is important. That is a sure sign of accomplishment.

AIM

དམིགས་ཡུལ།

One's aim should be self-existing wakefulness. Aim literally means the way you point your nose; it means one's birthplace, home or motherland. So, turn your nose toward home. Our home should be what is self-existing, free from concepts: primordial wakefulness.

ALL-ENCOMPASSING PURITY

དག་པ་རབ་འབྱམས།

Everything is all-encompassing purity; that is the Vajrayana perspective. However, this does not mean to think that something truly impure is pure.

ༀ

Training in all-encompassing purity is training in what is. Based on this perspective, one can apply Vajrayana practice authentically. Without this, visualization practice becomes just 'brick-laying' or mental labor.

ༀ

All that appears and exists actually is all-encompassing purity. We really should understand that everything — all world-systems and all beings, whatever appears and exists, the 'perceived' and the 'perceiver' — originates out of the sphere of the three kayas, takes place within the sphere of the three kayas, and dissolves back again into the sphere of the three kayas.

ༀ

Once we fully realize the state of rigpa by training again and again, the five elements are realized to be as they truly are in essence — the five female buddhas. The five aggregates are, in their natural state, the five male buddhas. At that point, you can truly declare that everything is all-encompassing purity.

ॐ

APOLOGY

བཤགས་པ།

Any misdeed, obscuration, violation or breach can be purified by apologizing from the bottom of your heart and resolving never to commit the transgression again. This must take place before three years have passed; otherwise, it is very difficult. This is the only good quality of evil deeds: they can be purified through apology and resolution. It is said that the buddhas are both skillful and compassionate in teaching the vajra vehicle of Secret Mantra. This implies that there is the possibility of purification through apology and resolution.

The misdeeds and obscurations created through countless past lives must be purified through apology, otherwise there is no way they will disappear by themselves. These negative patterns lie dormant as habitual tendencies that will eventually manifest in our dualistic frame of mind. We must purify them with apology, which is always possible, as I mentioned when defining the only good quality of evil deeds. This is the purpose of including the Hundred-Syllable Mantra among the preliminary practices. We apologize not only for the negative actions we have committed within this life and in this body, but for all the negative actions we have committed since beginningless time until now.

৯

According to the vajra vehicle of Secret Mantra, there is immense danger in being careless about one's samayas. However, when sincerely and genuinely mending a breach with apology and resolution, the damage is similar to a dent in a golden vessel; it can easily be repaired.

৯

APPEARANCE, INCREASE, AND ATTAINMENT

 སྣང་མཆེད་ཐོབ་གསུམ།

When someone dies, the subtle dissolution stage is comprised of the three experiences of appearance, increase, and attainment. These occur when the outer breath has stopped, but the inner breath — the inner circulation of energy-currents — has not yet ceased. For most people these three experiences do not last very long — just one, two, three. The redness experience is like the red light of the setting sun spreading across one's vision. The whiteness is like moonlight, and the blackness is like everything going completely dark. At the moment the white and red elements converge at the heart center, one experiences the unity of bliss and emptiness and either falls unconscious, or, if one is a practitioner who has familiarity with the state of rigpa, one experiences the ground luminosity of full attainment, the basic state of primordial purity.

The first of these four phases, appearance, is called the experience of whiteness, in which the white element obtained from our father descends from the crown of the head down towards the heart center. This is accompanied by the dissolution of the thirty-three types of aggressive thought states. The next experience is increase or the experience of redness, which takes place when the red element obtained from our mother ascends from below the navel up to the heart center. It is accompanied by the dissolution of the forty types of thought states linked to desire. The meeting of the red and white elements is called attainment or the experience of blackness, and is accompanied by the dissolution of the seven thought states of stupidity. All the eighty innate thought states cease when the red and white elements meet at the heart center. Ordinary people who have not recognized rigpa have no experience of or familiarity with a state that is awake, yet free from conceptual thought. They experience a blackout at this moment, becoming blank and unconscious.

ATTITUDE

ཀུན་སློང་།

Everything depends on whether one's intent is good or evil. To reach enlightenment we must pass through the paths and bhumis. Progress depends on pure attitude and good heart. Without pure attitude, all paths lead in a perverted direction.

It is not enough to strive for the higher teachings and ignore the real substance of the Dharma, which is a change in attitude. Unless we can change our hearts at a deep and profound level, the samsaric traits of our personality will all remain and we will still be seduced by appearances. As long as our mind is fickle, it is easy to become carried away in the chase for power and wealth or the pursuit of beautiful objects, in concerns of business and politics, in intrigues and deceit. It is easy to become an insensitive practitioner who cannot be 'cured' or changed by the Dharma.

BARDO

The general teachings outline six bardos. Two of these, the bardo of meditation and the bardo of dreaming, occur within the bardo of this life, which is defined as the period following birth until the onset of death. The actual process of passing away is called the bardo of dying. The bardo of dharmata occurs immediately after death, with the cessation of the outer and inner breath. Finally, the process of the consciousness seeking a new rebirth is called the bardo of becoming.

The most important thing is how we apply the teachings of the six bardos to our own practice. Most vital is the present instant of recognizing rigpa, the awakened state.

The most important thing is how we apply the teachings of the six bardos to our own practice. Most vital is the present instant of recognizing rigpa, the awakened state.

To prepare for the bardo state, it is very important to always keep in mind that, "Whatever I experience right now, whatever happens, is unreal, illusory." Such training will make it much easier to remember the same thing during the bardo states. The most crucial point, however, is to resolve on and rest in the state of rigpa, the nature of mind. Whether the world turns upside down or inside out, it does not matter: just lean back and rest in rigpa. We do not have to pigeonhole every single little experience that takes place as being such-and-such, because there is no end to the ideas that dualistic mind can create. It is not at all necessary to categorize. It is more important to simply resolve to recognize rigpa no matter what occurs.

BIRTH AND DEATH

From the point of view of ultimate truth, the acts of dying, taking rebirth, and experiencing this life are nothing more than superficial reality, relative truth.

The teachings on ultimate truth never mention that the buddha nature died or was reborn. The nature of mind, which is, in fact, the state of the primordial buddha Samantabhadra, is beyond birth and death. But sentient beings within the dream state of samsaric existence do experience the illusion of death and rebirth, so, in that sense, there is death and rebirth.

ༀ

BLESSINGS
བྱིན་རླབས།

What people usually consider blessings are what I would call superficial blessings. Often when you have something you want to get rid of, you ask, "Please bless me to be free from what I don't like." This can be sickness, pain, or an attack by evil spirits. It can also be as mundane as one's business not going so well, and so on. People ask for protection cords to wear around their necks, sacred medicine to eat, maybe a ritual to be performed. When they are cured, when the evil spirits have been repelled, the business is going well again, or whatever, they will say, "I got the blessings." These are known as conventional or superficial blessings. On the other hand, true blessings are the oral instructions on how to become enlightened in a single lifetime, which you can receive from a qualified master.

ༀ

BODHICHITTA

བྱང་ཆུབ་ཀྱི་སེམས།

By knowledge (*prajña*) alone or means (*upaya*) alone one will not get enlightened. By compassion alone, without emptiness, it is also somewhat difficult. Emptiness, unembraced by compassion, is not the perfect path and one's Dharma will stray onto the wrong track of self-interest.

Bodhichitta is the essence of both the Sutra and the Tantra teachings and its essence is compassion. In fact, relative compassion is called the path. Ultimate compassion is the fruition, which is the view, the perfect samadhi, and therefore the ultimate bodhichitta.

When realizing the perfect view, then the nature, the cognizant aspect, will manifest as compassion. It is never the case that, after attaining enlightenment, the buddhas leave sentient beings behind. This is due to the power of compassion. The link between buddhas and beings is made out of compassion.

Compassion does manifest spontaneously when resting in awareness. It is said that the expression arises as compassion. Although it is taught that compassion should be unartificial, uncontrived, in the beginning it is necessary to fabricate slightly.

BUDDHA

སངས་རྒྱས།

In Tibetan the term for 'buddha' is *sangye* which literally means 'purified perfection'. Dualistic consciousness tainted with the five poisons is purified, while the innate abundance of wisdom qualities is perfected. This is also called 'awakening' or 'enlightenment'.

It is important to transcend both limitations of existence and peace — neither resting in nirvanic peace nor straying into samsaric existence. Buddha means being liberated from both existence and peace.

The qualities of an enlightened buddha are not *his* qualities; they are the qualities of the buddha nature fully manifest. We also possess that same potential, but it is hidden, lying dormant.

The real buddha is the nature of our mind. Right now, our buddha nature is covered by obscurations that we need to purify. We also need to gather the two accumulations of merit and wisdom. A practice in which we think that the buddha is outside of ourselves, while ignoring the buddha within, will, by itself, never bring complete enlightenment. If we expect an external buddha up there in the sky to give us all the common and supreme accomplishments, we are merely placing our hopes in an outer object. The ultimate deity is within our own mind. We attain enlightenment by recognizing our true nature and training in that recognition.

The difference between buddhas and sentient beings lies in the latter's narrowness of scope or attitude. The reason all sentient beings confine themselves to their own little area of samsara is their limited attitude and thinking; that is what does it.

Right now, our awareness is fragmented. It is said that the mind of a sentient being is like a fragment of the sky. Whereas the mind of the buddhas is like the oneness of space, without one space during the day and another at night. There is neither a day nor a night space, nor such distinctions as yesterday's sky and to-day's sky. Sky has no such division as past and present. It is oneness, a continuum.

The difference between buddhas and sentient beings is only the difference between the narrowness and the openness of space. Sentient beings are like the open sky held within a tightly closed fist, while buddhas are fully open, all-encompassing.

॰

BUDDHAHOOD
སངས་རྒྱས་ཀྱི་གོ་འཕང་།

There is only one buddhahood, one awakened state, one ultimate destination. The true essence of buddha-hood is undivided empty cognizance suffused with knowing. This is also the basic nature of your own mind. The undivided empty cognizance, suffused with knowing is the same for a follower of Sakya, Gelug, Nyingma or Kagyü — they all have to enter the same path to enlightenment. Various types of true enlightenment do not exist, only different words, with the same meaning.

ॐ

There is a difference between being deluded and undeluded, between recognizing and not recognizing our nature. Although we have the essence of buddhahood within us, it is temporarily obscured. The primordially unmistaken quality is called enlightenment, buddhahood, the awakened state of dharmakaya. The primordially deluded aspect is called ignorance, the deluded experience of sentient beings.

ॐ

The awakened state is free of thought, yet vividly awake. If we train in this steadily and gradually, it becomes the fully awakened state, buddhahood.

ॐ

BUDDHA NATURE

In Tibetan the word for buddha nature is *deshek nyingpo*. *Deshek* or 'buddha' refers to all tathagatas and sugatas, the awakened ones, while *nyingpo* is the essential nature. Just as the essence of milk is butter, the essence of all buddhas is the state of realization.

Buddha nature is the very thing practiced in each of the nine vehicles, but how it is put into practice differs, because there is a refinement of understanding that becomes progressively more subtle through the vehicles.

The variety of teachings does not change the fact that the very essence of the Dharma, buddha nature, is extremely simple and easy. In fact, this essence is so simple and easy that sometimes it is hard to trust!

Our originally enlightened essence contains, within itself, the awakened state of all buddhas as the three aspects of vajra body, vajra speech and vajra mind. These three vajras are intrinsically contained within the

25

profound state of samadhi, which is none other than one's own nature. This fact is the starting point or source of the excellent main part beyond concepts.

༦

When the buddha nature that is present in everyone is depicted as being outside of ourselves in the form of a blue buddha, our buddha nature is named Samanta-bhadra, the dharmakaya buddha. When it is described as simply being present in everyone, it is called buddha nature.

༦

BUDDHA SHAKYAMUNI
ཤཱཀྱ་ཐུབ་པ།

The nature of our own mind, our buddha nature itself, is the dharmakaya buddha. Because we fail to acknowledge this fact, the dharmakaya has to manifest in visible forms for us to be able to understand what our own nature actually is. Therefore, the dharmakaya appears in a form like Buddha Shakyamuni, who demonstrates to us, "Recognize your mind! This is what your nature really is!" And he explains how the buddha nature is. Out of incredible compassion and with skillful means, the buddhas appear to put us on the right track.

ॐ

CAPACITY

ཐུགས་རྗེ།

Rigpa has a certain capacity. Capacity means the venue or the unobstructed medium for experience.

ॐ

Capacity is simply the unblocked basis for experience to take place.

ॐ

COGNIZANCE — LUMINOSITY

གསལ་བ་དང་འོད་གསལ།

The real meaning of luminosity is a lucid knowing. It is awareness free from darkness. This does not involve intellectualizing, as one's awareness is cognizant from the beginning; cognizant self-awareness is beyond conceptual mind.

In thoughtfree awareness, fixation on both subject and object have collapsed. Cognizance, however, does not cease.

༃

Didn't the Buddha say that mind in itself has no form, no sound, no smell, no taste, no texture, no dharmas? Here, *dharma* means mental object. He did not call it empty or void, he called it emptiness. This *-ness* means the same as the *ta* in the word *dharmata*, or in *tathata*. This word *ta* refers to being cognizant, and that is what we should understand as its meaning.

What the Buddha said exactly was that mind is the unity of empty cognizance. It is not said that space is emptiness; space is merely empty. This is how to discriminate between space and mind: space is empty and mind is emptiness. This word 'ta' is also used in dharmata, sameness, suchness. This suffix *-ness* always refers back to the cognizant wakefulness. You never say that awareness is empty, you always say that it is emptiness.

In short, awareness is not only empty, it can also know. This knowing is the cognizant nature when you speak about empty essence, cognizant nature — it is not some brilliant light like a light bulb. Do not un-

28

derstand it like that. What it means is a sense of being present like the vivid quality of being wide awake. It is empty of any identity, yet it is naturally awake and not limited to being one or the other; it is not an either-or situation.

COMPETITIVENESS

འགྲན་སེམས།

In Dharma practice be free from anger and competitiveness. If one cultivates resentment and rivalry through the Dharma, it is like Gampopa's famous saying: "If the Dharma is not practiced as it should be, it can become a cause for rebirth in the lower realms."

CONDITIONED, UNCONDITIONED

འདུས་བྱས་འདུས་མ་བྱས།

Everything is grouped into relative and ultimate, into conditioned and unconditioned. The conditioned is relative, the unconditioned is the ultimate. The conditioned is conceivable. You can talk about it, explain it. The unconditioned is inconceivable.

ತ

We can only partially hint at the inconceivable nature through words. We can hint at it with terms like primordial purity and spontaneous presence; but it is through practice that we actually experience that which is inconceivable.

ತ

Mastery over the conditioned can benefit a present situation. When we arrive in the bardo, the aggregates and elements collapse, then only the unconditioned can help you.

ತ

As long as the conditioned habitual patterns obscure the unconditioned, we do not experience our inconceivable nature of original wakefulness. So, now we have to grow familiar with the unconditioned, there is no other way.

ತ

CONDUCT

When people know that an individual has stepped onto the spiritual path, there is an accompanying responsibility. If later this person turns back and gives it up, that action destroys the pure perception in others and may even ruin their connection to the Dharma. Thus, it is better to begin slowly and progress gradually on the path, rather than to start out brilliantly and later become jaded and insensitive.

The practice we have, of first recognizing the view, training in the meditation, acting out of this view as the conduct and realizing the view fully as fruition — these are like the special chemicals that clean dirt from gold. In other words, view, meditation and conduct remove our confusion.

To lose the view in the conduct means to always be involved in accepting and rejecting, to entertain notions of something that needs to be attained and something that needs to be left behind. On the other hand, to lose the conduct in the view means to think that there is nothing to accept or reject — that whatever you do does not matter, and that there is no good and no evil. That is an even greater mistake.

One's behavior has to be in harmony with worldly standards. However, Dharma mixed with worldly work is not the perfect Dharma, I am sorry to say. Dharma and worldly aims are a contradiction, so keep those two things separate and distinct in your mind. In short, you need to distinguish between view and conduct. The view is free from hope and fear. The conduct is with hope and fear.

ॐ

CONFIDENCE
གདེངས།

Until you realize the correct view, it is very difficult to have true self-confidence. No matter how much one tries to act self-assured, it is only an intellectual patch.

True confidence comes from realizing the view.

ॐ

CONFUSION

འཁྲུལ་པ།

Delusion is like becoming possessed during a
séance; a spirit inhabits someone's body so that he suddenly hops around and does all kinds of crazy things.
This is what has happened in the case of sentient
beings. Possessed by the 'spirit' of ignorance and the
84,000 disturbing emotions, they have been dancing
around and doing incredible things. They have under-
gone all different kinds of pain and misery for so long,
aeons and aeons. But their possession is self-created. It
is not something from outside. Their buddha nature
has lost track of itself and created samsara. It is also
buddha nature which, recognizing itself, clears up the
delusion of samsaric existence; it does not come from
outside. The moment of recognizing is like the spirit
leaving. One had lost control of oneself and been
dancing around when all of a sudden the possession
vanishes. We cannot even say where it went. This is
called the 'collapse of confusion'.

ॐ

Clinging ties us to samsara. Obscurations are primordially nonexistent; confusion is momentary. Sam-

sara is actually a repeated momentary incident. Confusion and samsara are synonyms.

༄

In last night's dream, there was joy and sorrow, houses and palaces and so forth. We can dream of all these things, but when we wake up whatever we dreamt is nonexistent. Likewise, right now for ordinary beings, all phenomena definitely exist due to the power of confusion. But when we are not confused, when we have attained stability in the wisdom of all the buddhas, as a sign that phenomena are primordially nonexistent, we can traverse freely through everything. If all these phenomena were primordially existing, the buddhas would have to annihilate them in order to traverse freely through them, but that is not the case.

༄

Through becoming stable in rigpa, we realize that whatever we perceived was delusion that we ourselves created. It was a deluded personal experience.

༄

When we forget mind essence we become distracted and confusion arises.

Nondualistic wakefulness destroys dualistic fixation. When dualistic fixation collapses then deluded experience falls apart and the cause and effect of karma, habitual tendencies and all conceptual activity are destroyed or fall way.

ॐ

An important principle in Vajrayana is that the confused state of mind can be its own best remedy.

ॐ

CONSCIOUSNESS
རྣམ་ཤེས།

To be conscious and cognizant are the characteristics of consciousness. It has cognizance, it does know — but not the three times simultaneously. Dualistic consciousness is like a dog; it only notices what is exactly in front of it. Likewise the wakefulness of grasping mind cannot simultaneously know what is in front, in the middle, and in the back, i.e. the three times. Whereas, the wakefulness of rigpa can know the three times simultaneously.

ॐ

CONTINUITY

Rigpa is by itself completely awake. It is the unity of being cognizant and empty suffused with awareness. As long as it is not deteriorated or lost, we do not need to think we should avoid being distracted. To maintain the continuity means to not lose rigpa. To 'maintain' does not mean to prolong or make it last, which would be conceptual. The essential point is 'not losing the continuity'. Once we lose the continuity, we have become distracted. To not lose the continuity is to remain undistracted.

DAKINI SCRIPT

མ་བན་འགྲོའི་བརྡ་ཡིག

Dakini letters are symbolic script. Only a *tertön* can perceive their meaning — no one else. He decodes the secret writing, meaning that he writes it out in understandable letters. Even if he makes a spelling mistake, the terma letters will remain in his experience until he notices there is a mistake, rectifies it and continues. That is why a genuine terma is always correct.

༅

DEITIES

People expect that after reciting a certain number of mantras, the deity will arrive in front of them for their eyes to see. Actually, that attitude externalizes the deity. The ultimate deity is the unity of emptiness and cognizance, the nature of your own mind. Instead of ringing a bell and beating a drum, expecting the deity to appear up there in the sky before you, you should simply recognize what it is that imagines all this. Then, you will see the state in which emptiness and cognizance are indivisible. That is to be face-to-face with the real deity. Isn't that much easier than hoping a deity will appear from the outside? The real vision of the deity is to recognize the nature of your mind.

༅

To recognize mind essence captures the life-force of thousands of buddhas. When you take hold of the life-force, they cannot escape you. Through the power of samadhi, you capture the life-force of all the deities, without having to conjure them up as being somewhere over there in the distance.

To accomplish a deity, you must know the nature of the deity you are trying to accomplish. This is called 'identifying the deity to be accomplished'. The names, colors and attributes may differ, but a deity is actually the unity of primordial purity and spontaneous presence. In this way, development and completion are also contained within Trekchö and Tögal.

DEMONS

དུད།

The first of the four demons is the demon of the Lord of Death, which cuts our life short. Second is the demon of the physical aggregates, which prevents the attainment of the rainbow body. Third is the demon of the disturbing emotions, the three poisons that prevent liberation from samsara. Finally, there is the demon of the son of the gods, which is distraction in the meditation state and the tendency to postpone practice. Procrastination is the demon of the son of the gods, which creates obstacles for samadhi.

৯

The real demon, however, is our conceptual thinking. Falling into conceptualization is the real demon. By recognizing our mind essence, all demons are defeated; the four *maras* are vanquished and all obstacles are obliterated.

৯

DEVELOPMENT AND
COMPLETION STAGES

བསྐྱེད་རྫོགས།

The main purpose of development stage is to destroy our clinging to the accepted belief in a solid reality. It is our fixation on concreteness that makes us continue in samsaric existence. The development stage dismantles such fixation. We do this by imagining the world to be a buddhafield, our dwelling place the celestial palace, and the beings in it the divine forms of deities, visible yet intangible like a rainbow in the sky.

❧

The development stage is like awakening from the dream state, it is manifesting what primordially exists. The purpose is to purify evil deeds, to prevent one's thinking from falling under the influence of the disturbing emotions. Some people have so much thought activity that only development stage is useful and completion stage cannot yet benefit them. They may think, "What is the use of simply remaining! There is nothing nor anybody to see. It would be better to have something to think of." Many people have this attitude. Ordinary thought activity can be quite difficult to handle. When there are many thoughts, the disturbing emotions accumulate karma, so if one can instead think of the celestial palace, the deity and so forth, the thoughts are utilized without gathering karma and evil deeds.

❧

Do not consider development stage to involve imagining something that is not real, like pretending that a piece of wood is pure gold. Development stage is not at all like that. It is a way to simply acknowledge what already is, what already exists. Development stage means to mentally create or imagine the form of the buddhas. Although visualization is at this point an artificial construct, a mentally fabricated act, still it is an imitation that resembles what is already present in us. Until we are able to practice the ultimate development stage, we need to visualize or mentally create pure images in order to approach that absolute state.

The ordinary development stage is a likeness or imitation of the real thing. Although it's a resemblance and not the real thing, it's not exactly false, because development stage is a valid exercise in seeing things as they actually are, rather than as something other. Completion stage is the true view, the natural state.

Development stage is spontaneous presence and completion stage is primordial purity. The crucial point here is that primordial purity and spontaneous presence are indivisible. The development stage is what primordially exists within oneself: the intrinsic essence that is primordially pure and its nature that is spontaneously present. Actually, the real root of development stage is the nature of spontaneous presence.

ॐ

It is not the case that one imagines something that did not already exist, like raising someone from the dead, and that the deities suddenly appear at the end. The expression of the spontaneously present nature from the essence of primordial purity is there from the beginning, so development and completion stage are to be practiced as a unity.

ॐ

Development stage is not something false; it is not self-deception, because primordial purity is naturally endowed with spontaneously present qualities. These are the qualities of rigpa, of nondual awareness. If our nature were merely empty, there would be no qualities at all. Instead, it is empty while being an original wakefulness, and the qualities of this wakefulness are inconceivable. This aspect of wakefulness means that original knowing is never lost, even though for us original emptiness may seem to be without such wakefulness.

It is not possible to attain enlightenment by development stage alone if it is not embraced by completion stage.

ॐ

The authentic way of practicing development stage is to allow the visualization to unfold as the natural expression of rigpa. If one wants to practice a perfect development stage it is impossible without being introduced to awareness.

ॐ

Without moving away from the state of nondual awareness, the expression of awareness arises as the development stage. That is the ideal. In fact, the two — development and completion — need not be separate. Remain in awareness and let the expression of awareness arise as the development stage; that is the perfect development and completion stage.

ॐ

Development stage is the profound method that enables us in one lifetime and in one body to attain enlightenment through deity, mantra and samadhi.

Completion stage means that the deity is none other than our originally enlightened buddha nature.

৯

The real development stage should unfold within the samadhi of suchness, like a reflection appearing in a bright mirror. When the reflection of a *tangka* appears, the mirror does not lose its brightness. In other words, do not leave the completion stage behind in order for the development stage to take place. Otherwise, development stage becomes construction work, like making something out of clay or wood. Can a tangka be reflected in a piece of wood?

৯

The development stage can take place while recognizing mind essence, since the expression of awareness is unobstructed. If the essence were obstructed the development stage could not arise, but it is not so. The development stage is allowed to develop, to manifest, without harming the primordial purity one bit. Without moving away from unchanging primordial purity, the spontaneous presence, the expression of awareness, can manifest. This is because of the indivisibility of primordial purity and spontaneous presence.

DEVOTION, COMPASSION

དད་པ་དང་སྙིང་རྗེ།

It is not enough to just say, "Things are empty, mind is empty, everything is empty." It is not enough to only think rigpa. One needs to gather the accumulations, purify negative karmas and receive the blessings of the glorious guru. It is said that to depend on other methods than these should be known as delusion. By other methods, one will not realize rigpa.

Devotion to all the buddhas above means to all the enlightened lineage masters from dharmakaya Samantabhadra down to your own guru. Compassion for all sentient beings below means for all the six kinds of beings who have been one's mother. These two — devotion and compassion — are like your head and your feet. By heart alone you are not a whole human being. Never say, "Only rigpa, only rigpa, I do not need devotion or compassion." That is not the authentic way to practice.

༄

The special quality of Buddhism is, at best, to recognize emptiness, the mind essence, but if not, you should definitely practice compassion. Anyone can cultivate compassion. As I have mentioned before, imagine your mother is in front of you and then some enemies come and cut off her arms, legs and head — how would you feel? That is called compassion. It is an overwhelming feeling. For example, especially if you are incapable or are tied down with chains and ropes and your mother is dragged in front of you. The enemies arrive and first they pull out her eyes, strangle her and finally take out her heart. How would you feel? You would feel love and compassion. Through the blessing or virtue of this compassion, emptiness will dawn within your being.

The precious relative bodhichitta is compassion and the precious ultimate bodhichitta is emptiness. With compassion and emptiness, enlightenment is unavoidable. All the sutras, tantras, scriptures and oral instructions are contained within this. It is not all right to say, "I don't need devotion, I don't need compassion for beings, just meditation is sufficient." With compassion and emptiness, the view is automatically like a blazing fire. When this happens the profound emptiness, self-existing wakefulness, very quickly arises in one's being. This is unfailing, unfabricated, unobscured, the straight path for attaining enlightenment within rigpa.

ॐ

What is the supreme method or means? It is devotion and compassion. In the beginning, you need a fabricated devotion, a natural unfabricated devotion will not happen right away. It is also said that uncontrived compassion does not occur immediately. How do you do it? As you get more and more stable in awareness, you will feel, "Sentient beings are unaware of this most precious thing, which is like the Buddha in the palm of my hand." Naturally, you will feel compassion toward sentient beings, that is how it will be. And devotion is like this, "How fantastic to have received teachings on how to cut through the very basis and root of confusion. It is incredible, this perfection of all virtues, exhaustion of all faults. There is nothing superior to this awareness!" This is how you gain trust and confidence. The devotion and compassion that does not need to be fabricated is present within this awareness, in your own essence.

ॐ

DHARMA PRACTICE
ཆོས་ཀྱི་ཉམས་ལེན།

To practice the Dharma means, chiefly, to nurture the qualities of trust, diligence and insight. Trust is to have confidence in the teachings and the one who taught them — in the Buddha and the Sangha, the upholders of the teachings. Diligence is what carries you through to completion. Insight is the outcome of listening to teachings, thinking about them and applying them. When you hear something and you gain confidence in it, then you have insight, which is the knowledge resulting from learning. Thinking it over, you gain the knowledge from reflection. Finally, there is the knowledge acquired through meditation practice.

The whole point of Dharma practice is to remove the clouds and allow the actualization of what already is — the awakened state of mind, the buddha nature. The nature of our mind is primordially pure, primordially enlightened. The way to remove our two obscurations is to train in conditioned virtue and apply the unconditioned training in original wakefulness, i.e. the two accumulations.

DILIGENCE
བརྩོན་འགྲུས།

The diligence of practice is said to be like the string of a bow. First the string is slack but when the bow is strung, the string stays continuously taut. Diligence should be like a river flowing downwards — unceasing and unforced. It does not help to be tense or forceful, which is only necessary when carrying a load.

The difference between buddhas and sentient beings is diligence. If you are very diligent, you can become a buddha, if not you remain a sentient being.

DISCIPLE
སློབ་མ།

Where I come from, when we say 'disciple' it means someone who gives up everything and focuses one-pointedly on attaining enlightenment in that same body and lifetime. Anyone else, who merely receives a couple of empowerments, teachings or a reading transmission now and then, is not necessarily counted as a 'full-time practicing disciple'.

꙳

DISTRACTION
རྣམ་གཡེང་།

It is crucial to understand when there is distraction and when there is no distraction. While being distracted, one is not aware of it. It is only when finished being distracted that one thinks, "Oh, I was wandering."

꙳

DISTURBING EMOTIONS
ཉོན་མོངས་པ།

Every emotion is a thought, and any thought is the mind moving. When thinking, the attention moves towards one object, then towards another, then a third, right? The very root of emotion is your attention in motion. To cut the root of this movement you must recognize from where the attention moves.

꙳

There are three traditional methods of dealing with emotions: abandoning them, transforming them, and recognizing their nature. All three levels of Buddhist teaching, all three yanas, describe how to deal with disturbing emotions. It is never taught, on any level, that one can be an enlightened buddha while remaining involved in disturbing emotions — never. Each level deals with emotions differently.

Just like darkness cannot remain when the sun rises, none of the disturbing emotions can endure within the recognition of mind nature. That is the moment of realizing original wakefulness, and it is the same for each of the five poisons.

In any of the five disturbing emotions, we do not have to transmute the emotion into empty cognizance. The nature of the emotion *already is* this indivisible empty cognizance.

Recognition of the nature in actuality causes the disturbing emotion to simply vanish. This is the real path.

DOUBT
ཐེ་ཚོམ།

Anyone can have doubts. For example, some kind of suspicion that you get involved in such as, "Maybe what I understand is not really the ultimate, maybe there is something better, maybe there is something unchanging. My state is not unchanging, the guru has been talking about this state of rigpa, but this does not seem to be it. I wonder what this is? Maybe it's not the right thing!" Until you have truly established the natural state, no matter who you are, you will some-times begin to doubt.

DREAM

རྨི་ལམ།

Not recognizing mind essence is the same as dreaming. Dreaming is not primordial; it is momentary.

All dreams take place within the state of sleep, the framework of sleep. In the same way, all our pleasure and pain, hope and fear, whatever we experience right now during the waking state — the world, ourselves, and other people — all these take place within the framework of dualistic mind. All the drama and display of dualistic mind is the unaware reflection of the buddha nature. As long as we believe that the experiences of dualistic mind are real, we wander endlessly in samsaric existence. This is not the case with the primordial Buddha Samantabhadra. He never fell asleep to begin with, so how could he have any dreams?

Sleep is only a subsidiary of ignorance; the real stupidity is not knowing our own awareness wisdom. The most essential Buddhist training is all about recognizing this basic nature, training in the strength of that recognition, and finally attaining complete stability. That is the only way to awaken from this dream state.

DUALITY

Although the basic original state of self-existing wakefulness has no duality whatsoever, seeming duality takes place because of fixating upon experience as being something other.

Dualistic fixation should be destroyed. That is the whole reason why we strive so diligently in meditation to recognize mind essence. *Yeshe* means original knowing. We grow used to original knowing by recognizing our essence as primordial purity. Nondual wakefulness destroys fixation on duality. When dualistic fixation is destroyed, deluded experience falls apart and conceptual activity collapses. This is what we should resolve upon and become completely clear about.

We need to let go of dualistic mind. What is left over is unconfined nondual awareness. Non-clinging awareness is already present the moment you recognize rigpa; it is there for everyone. Unfortunately, sentient beings do not know how to look — and they do not trust it even if they do see.

Enlightenment is never attained as long as duality remains. As long as we have these two — to get rid of one thing and attain another — duality remains. Everything must become oneness in the recognition of mind essence; then there is no duality.

DZOGCHEN

All buddhas teach Dzogchen, but never in as open a way as during the reign of Buddha Shakyamuni. During this period, even the word 'Dzogchen' is world-renowned and can be heard as far as the wind pervades. Despite their widespread nature, the teachings themselves, the pith instructions, are sealed with the stamp of secrecy.

ى

In Dzogchen all phenomena of samsara and nirvana are completed or perfected in the expanse of the single sphere of dharmakaya awareness. Dzogchen embodies completion or perfection in the sense that *dzog* means 'finished' — in other words, there's nothing further; it's done, over with, complete.

ى

The Dzogchen system emphasizes stripping awareness to its naked state. It does not teach clinging to emptiness in any way whatsoever.

ى

The Great Perfection is totally beyond pigeonholing anything in any way whatsoever. It is utterly open, beyond categories, limitations and the confines of assumptions and beliefs. All other ways of describing things are confined by categories and limitations.

ى

The special quality of Dzogchen is the view that is totally free from any ideas whatsoever. This view is called the *view of fruition*; it is utterly devoid of any conceptual formulations.

ৎ

In Dzogchen, the ultimate destination to arrive at is the view of the kayas and wisdoms.

ৎ

EIGHT ANALOGIES OF ILLUSION
སྒྱུ་མའི་དཔེ་བརྒྱད།

The eight analogies of illusion are: reflections in a mirror, the moon in water, echoes, rainbows, dreams, the city of Gandharvas, mirages, and the magical illusions created by a magician. They compare our experiences and perceptions to something that seems to truly be there but in reality is not. The solid character we usually attach to experience simply vanishes once its illusory nature is seen in actuality. That is how a great yogi can move freely through what other people see as solid matter.

ৎ

EMPOWERMENT

དབང་བསྐུར།

The main empowerments of the inner tantras are known as the four empowerments. The first, the vase empowerment, refers to Mahayoga. In Anu Yoga, there are two parts: through your own body and through the body of another. The empowerment to your own body is called the secret empowerment and the empowerment to the body of another is called the wisdom-knowledge empowerment. Finally, the fourth is called the precious word empowerment. The vajra master confers empowerment by means of these four, which are also called elaborate, unelaborate, very unelaborate and extremely unelaborate. These four empowerments are the basis of all Vajrayana teachings.

ॐ

EMPTINESS

སྟོང་པ་ཉིད།

All Buddhist systems of philosophy expound that things — phenomena and mind — are empty, as they have to. The intention of the Buddha when using the word 'emptiness' is that *-ness* is the cognizant quality, so emptiness here should be understood as 'empty cognizance'. Whenever the suffix *-ness* is included, we should understand its pure connotation. If we understand 'emptiness' as meaning just an empty voidness, rather than 'empty cognizance', we lean too much towards nihilism, the idea that everything is a big blank void. That would be a serious sidetrack.

ENEMIES

དགྲ་བོ།

There are three kinds of enemies. The external enemies are people who have a perverted view of and are hostile towards the teachings and practitioners. They say that there is no reason for compassion, no truth in the Dharma, no deities, no mantras, no blessings, and no buddha activity. The inner enemies are our conceptual thoughts of dualistic clinging — outwardly to the perceived objects and inwardly to the perceiving mind. The ultimate enemy is doubt and the concept of antidote, the cognitive obscuration.

ENHANCEMENT

 བོགས་འདོན།

Devotion and compassion strengthen the recognition of mind nature. To develop devotion to the enlightened ones and compassion for sentient beings are, therefore, enhancement practices.

ENLIGHTENMENT

བྱང་ཆུབ།

The enlightened state of a buddha perceives everything in all directions at the same moment and in a completely unobstructed fashion. The Dharma teachings are an expression arising from this state, and are totally free from any falsehood or pretense.

We are taught that we can achieve enlightenment by practicing Dharma, engaging in virtue and avoiding nonvirtue. This is because we have the potential — because our nature is potentially the state of enlightenment. A gold lodestone has the potential to yield gold when it is smelted, but a piece of wood does not because it does not have the nature of gold. We have the capacity for enlightenment because our nature is the enlightened essence.

ॐ

There are different levels of enlightenment. There is the enlightenment of an arhat, of a mahabodhisattva, and the true and complete enlightenment of a buddha. The five paths and the ten bhumis are progressive stages that gradually lead to true and complete enlightenment.

ॐ

The way to true and complete enlightenment is by unifying means and knowledge, which are great compassion and insight into emptiness. The unity of emptiness and compassion is the true path to the complete enlightenment of a buddha.

ॐ

To reach enlightenment, you need to directly experience the emptiness of mind. The awakened state, our own self-existing wakefulness, should not be fabricated or altered in any way at all. It is natural emptiness. *Empty* means free of visible form, sound, smell, taste or texture. The *-ness* is the knowing, cognizant quality. We need to see that this is so — that it is not only empty, but also naturally cognizant. And we need to not only see this and experience it, but also to grow used to it. Growing accustomed to this clears away obscurations, negative deeds and past karma, and destroys delusion at its root. That is how to become enlightened, and that is the root of blessings. Simply understanding what enlightenment is does not enlighten you.

ॐ

The way to become enlightened is to train in recognizing mind essence and becoming stable in this recognition.

ॐ

The road to Bodhgaya is not level; there are mountain passes, valleys, rivers, precipices and so forth. No matter what your personal road is like do not lose courage, but repeatedly relax loosely in nondual awareness. If we practice like this then one day, we will arrive in Bodhgaya, which means we will attain enlightenment. If we do not set out on the road, we will never arrive.

ॐ

The confusion that arose on the path stage can be cleared away. When we remove the temporary defilement from the primordially awakened state, we become re-enlightened instead of primordially enlightened. This is accomplished by following the oral instructions of a qualified master.

ॐ

Enlightenment is possible when a qualified master meets a worthy, receptive disciple who possesses the highest capacity, and transmits, or points out, the unmistaken essence of mind so that the disciple recognizes it. It can indeed be pointed out; it can indeed be recognized; and it can indeed be trained in. If the student practices this diligently, he or she can unquestionably attain complete enlightenment.

ॐ

Sentient beings do not experience the realm of true enlightenment. We attain the state of unexcelled enlightenment when at some stage we possess all the qualities and have purified all the obscurations. When the yogi attains accomplishment, there is no impure experience of sights, sounds or states of mind, not even as much as a mote of dust. Everything has become the continuity of pure wakefulness.

Enlightenment is like awakening from sleep. All the perceptions and phenomena experienced during the day are made by grasping mind. All that is experienced at night is made by sleep. When awakening from sleep there is nothing left of the dream. When the perceptions and experiences of deluded grasping mind have been completely purified; there is nothing left of these present confused experiences. When phenomena manifest, they are the display of rainbow light. If there is no manifestation, it is simply the space of primordial purity.

ERRORS
གོལ་བོར།

During the path stage, we sometimes lose control because of not recognizing our nature, due to our habitual patterns, and falling under the influence of anger and passion. While distracted, the essence seems obstructed, as if there were some interruption, but in the view of the true yogi, original wakefulness is completely beyond waxing and waning.

"Mara lies in ambush along the path of distraction." Like this saying, distraction is our worst enemy. If you wander away, the essence seems lost.

Once you have recognized nondual awareness, there is absolutely no point in distracting yourself. Once you have recognized awareness the most important point is to not wander off.

To train in thinking, "I am undistracted, undistracted, undistracted," is like a person who is not bound by an iron chain, but is still tied down by a golden chain. However, it is more serious to not even have the thought, "I am distracted." One is totally under the influence of unbridled thoughts, which is like being tied with an iron chain. One needs to cast away both the thoughts, "I am distracted," as well as "I am undistracted."

One might have recognized mind essence, but the important point is to resolve on it. Otherwise, one is still fettered and unable to be free. In the first moment after noticing that one is distracted one thinks, "I was distracted." That is the occurrence of effortful mindfulness. To then think, "I shouldn't be distracted," is to add a second thought. In the moment of noticing, "I was distracted," neither accept nor reject, and you arrive directly in awareness, like a flashlight the moment it is switched on. This is an important point.

When clung to, the three experiences of bliss, clarity and nonthought are dispositions of dualistic mind. When not grasped they are the qualities of the three kayas and when grasped they result in the three realms of samsara.

ESSENCE

ངོ་བོ།

The essence is like the original sun shining: naturally radiant and unformed.

၈

"Recognize mind essence, recognize mind essence," it is said. Once we get familiar with that essence, it will conquer all karmas, habitual patterns and deluded experiences. It is sufficient unto itself.

၈

Understand it in this way: although beings have similar qualities, we are not one. We have the same essence, which is empty and cognizant, but our form of manifestation is separate and distinct from that of another sentient being.

၈

EXPERIENCE

སྒོམ་བ།

Intellectual understanding is the idea that all phenomena are empty and devoid of a self-entity. A true yogi simply stays in the mountains and after reflecting on this directly experiences the awakened state. There are three steps: intellectual understanding, experience and realization. The experience is when you have resolved that rigpa is empty; that it is beyond arising, dwelling and ceasing. The actual practice, however, is expressed by the words, "Don't wander, don't be distracted!" Without applying the meaning of words, we remain in indifference.

Experience only occurs in a direct way, in practical reality; not as a theory or an idea of what something is like. If our spiritual practice or meditation is merely an exercise in imagining or keeping a 'thing' in mind, it is only a theory, and not immediate experience.

EXPERIENCE, EXPERIENCES

ཉམས་སྣང་དང་ཉམས་སྣང་།

What we call a hell is merely a perception. It is an experience. Everything we experience now is perception. Therefore, it is said, "Objects are only perceptions without any true existence." Besides being perceived, objects do not possess any concrete existence, not as much as even a speck of dust. Think deeply about this: they are experience; they do not really exist.

༷

Appearances can only exist if there is a mind that beholds them. The 'beholding' of an appearance is nothing other than experience; that is what actually takes place. Without a perceiving mind, how could an appearance be an appearance? It would not exist anywhere. Perceptions are experienced by mind; water or earth does not experience them. All objects vividly appear as long as the mind apprehends them. But they are a mere presence, simply an appearance. It is mind that apprehends this mere presence. When this mind does not apprehend, hold onto, or fixate upon what is experienced — in other words, when the real, authentic samadhi of suchness dawns within your stream-of-being — then 'reality' loses its solid, obstructing quality. That is why accomplished yogis cannot be burnt, drowned, or harmed by wind. Since fixation has disintegrated from within, in their experience, all appearances are a mere presence.

There are two kinds of experiences, pleasant and unpleasant. These are all signs of practice. Not all signs of practice are enjoyable. But no matter what happens, understand that all experiences are like mere clouds within the sky of primordial purity. The sky sometimes has clouds; sometimes it is free from clouds. Sometimes it rains, storms and snows, which are the unpleasant experiences. Sometimes, there are pleasant experiences with no clouds, but instead sunshine and rainbows, yet still these are only experiences.

Whatever experiences occur, either good or bad, you should regard them like an old man watching children play: free from hope and fear; remain in stable awareness.

The Buddha initially taught that all things are empty. This was unavoidable; indeed, it was justifiable, because we need to dismantle our fixation on the permanence of what we experience. A normal person clings to experiences as solid, as being 'that' — not just as mere experience, but something which has solidity, is real, concrete. Honestly, look at what happens: experience is simply experience. It is not made out of anything whatsoever. In reality, it has no form, no sound, no color, no taste and no texture.

When we begin to grow more stable in the absence of impure experiences, the manifestations of pure experience start to become an actuality, including all the qualities of deities, as well as all the aspects of wisdom.

While we are unenlightened, we have an element of shared experiences. The mountains, the city, the roads, the sky, the five elements, all appear to unenlightened beings as being solid and truly existing. Right now, we have impure experience: constantly solidifying the content of experience into a solid reality. That is the definition of 'impure'. But it does not have to remain like that.

჻

EXPRESSION

རྩལ།

When you do not recognize the essence of your own expression it takes the form of perceiver and perceived. The perceived is seen as external, 'there', the perceiver as being 'here'.

჻

When the essence in the expression is not recognized, the expression takes the form of dualistic thinking.

჻

When the expression of rigpa recognizes itself, it arises as knowledge, *prajña*. This is not the ordinary knowledge that is the outcome of learning, reflecting and meditating. It is the real *prajñaparamita*, transcendent knowledge. The expression dissolves back and there is only awareness. That moment is identical with the state of primordial enlightenment of all buddhas, the state that never strayed from itself.

ॐ

FAULT

རང་སྐྱོན།

We need to acknowledge our faults to be able to remedy them; this is important.

ॐ

Always scrutinize your own shortcomings. Ignore the faults of others. Keep this attitude: "Whether they are pure or whether they are defiled, it is none of my business!" Be your own teacher; keep a strict check on yourself. That is sufficient! There is then no chance for a single error to sneak in.

ॐ

FEAST

ཚོགས་འབོར།

The word 'feast' in Tibetan is *tsok*, which means 'gathering' of many things. There are three kinds of gatherings: the 'majestic gathering of deities', the 'loyal gathering of human beings', loyal meaning having pure samaya, and the 'meritorious gathering of abundance', all kinds of non-poisonous food and drink.

෴

Feast offering is one of the best activities between sessions. It is the supreme way of accumulating merit, it fulfills all wishes and at the end of this life, you will arrive in the line of the vidyadharas. Feast offering is the king of all offerings.

෴

FIXATION

Someone who has pacified and purified the obstructing force of ego-fixation enjoys the elixir of Vajrayana teachings. Fixation slips in when we think that earth is merely earth, water is water, etc.. However, the fixation on concreteness falls apart when we consider that, "Earth is Buddha Lochana, water is Mamaki, fire is Pandaravasini, wind is Samayatara and space is the pure Dhatvishvari."

In order to be born in the hells there have to be two things, the place and the one who takes rebirth. When dualistic fixation has been destroyed and duality has become oneness, how can there be a place to take birth? The cause of the hells has then been emptied.

৽

When our clinging to appearances has been destroyed, they will be beyond benefit or harm.

৽

FOUR MIND-CHANGINGS

The most excellent body is the human body within the realm of desire, the *Kamaloka*. In the realm of desire, the emotions are quite strong, unlike in the gods' realms including the seventeen realms of form or in the four formless realms where the emotions are not very strong nor are the wisdoms or the antidotes. It is said, "The stronger the emotions, the stronger the wisdoms." When you have a fire if you only put on a little wood, the flames will only be quite small. If you put on a lot of wood, you will have a huge fire. The human body is said to be the most excellent, first class.

૭

We have been born in a place where it has been difficult to be born — the southern Jambu Continent; we have met the one who is difficult to meet — the great being, the qualified master; and we have obtained what is difficult to obtain — the sacred teachings. Thus, we now possess the threefold ease and being free from the three difficulties, we have obtained the precious human body. This possession is indispensable for the short path for attaining enlightenment in this very body and life.

૭

The starting point, the first step through the door to Dharma practice, is the understanding that life is impermanent, that our time is running out. Not taking impermanence to heart prevents our Dharma practice from being successful. Although we might think we do not have time for Dharma practice, is there anybody who has time to die?

૭

If the effect of an action were to manifest immediately, then even if someone said, "Please do a negative deed," there is no way we would do so because we would instantly see the result. If we have eyes and stand on the brink of an abyss, we will not jump, because we see that by jumping we would die. If we could see the effect of our good and evil actions, we would never commit negative actions. But this world is not like that; here, the results of our actions appear unclear and vague. If the result of a negative action would ripen the moment after enacting it, nobody would commit evil. Likewise, people would not hold back from positive deeds because the effect would be instantaneous. However, the results of actions do not ripen immediately; they are not instantly discernible, but only ripen slowly. Due to not realizing the positive and negative results of actions and not understanding impermanence, we are completely oblivious to the consequences of our actions. We do not see what is happening, we do not see how much or how little merit we have, so we walk around like stupid cows.

༈

The Buddha spoke of the ultimate view that cuts through the root of the three poisons. If we want to bring an end to samsaric existence and cross the ocean of samsaric pain and suffering, we need to practice the precious Dharma that the Buddha taught. If, on the other hand, we are happy and content to continue in the three realms of samsara and we are not tired of undergoing endless suffering, of course we do not need to practice the Dharma. If we think, "I've been circling around taking birth, growing old, getting sick, and dying, taking birth, growing old, getting sick, and dying again and again endlessly, and I'll just go on like that," we can certainly continue doing so, and we don't need to practice the Dharma.

ॐ

In Tibet, there is a saying, "When seen from afar, yaks look healthy and handsome; close up, they look like sickly sheep; but under their fleece, they are infested with lice and scabies." In other words, when we look at others from afar they may appear to have happiness, prestige, friends and wealth. But when we get closer, we see that they are not very happy and their situation is not ideal. There is always something to complain about, and when we get very close and examine their inner feelings, each person has his own set of worries and carries his own burden around with him. No one is in perfect happiness. That is why the Buddha called samsara an ocean of suffering, not an ocean of bliss.

FREEING
གྲོལ་བ།

Though one might have recognized the awakened state, thoughts will still inflict harm unless one understands how to free them. When remaining in awareness itself, every thought movement, no matter what kind, is like a drawing in air.

FRUITION
འབྲས་བུ།

There is, essentially, no difference whatsoever between ground and fruition. But the qualities are manifest at the time of fruition, whereas at the time of the ground they were not acknowledged. It is not that there are some new qualities that appear at the time of fruition. For example, the qualities of a flower are already in the seed. It has all the colors, the white, red, yellow, etc. However, can we say that the seed is the fruition state of a flower? No, we cannot, because the flower is not fully bloomed. Likewise, the qualities of the fruition are contained in the state of the ground. However they are not evident; they are not manifest. That is the difference between ground and fruition. The fruition will not appear unless one applies effort at the time of the path. That is the purpose of the path.

FUTILITY

སྙིང་པོ་མེད་པ།

To understand that whatever mundane activity we do, whatever we have done, is totally futile, that is true insight. That is real understanding. Nothing other than Dharma has any real value, any real substance. So, what next? Apply the Dharma! Apply it increasingly, and you will capture the stronghold of the view. That is the way to truly understand the Dharma. When we look closely at things around us and in ourselves, we should come to the understanding that everything we have done is basically useless. There is true understanding in realizing that "I have really fooled myself. Nobody else fooled me; I fooled myself."

಄

GREAT BLISS
བདེ་བ་ཆེན་པོ།

'Great bliss' does not mean some grand state of conditioned pleasure, but rather unconditioned bliss totally free of even the word 'pain'.

಄

HABITUAL TENDENCIES
བག་ཆགས།

Habitual tendencies are very subtle. The easiest way to understand this is through the example of the dream state. Whatever seemingly takes place while dreaming is the product of habitual tendencies and is nothing that we can take hold of. Nothing is tangible, yet everything can be experienced. When that kind of delusion occurs on a very subtle level it is due to habitual tendencies.

స

IGNORANCE
མ་རིག་པ།

There are two types of ignorance: coemergent and conceptual ignorance. In the moment after seeing our essence, it almost immediately slips away. We get distracted and we start to think of something. Coemergent ignorance is simply to forget. Conceptual ignorance comes in the moment after forgetting, forming thought after thought. As one thought follows after another, a long train of thoughts can develop. Forgetting and thinking — that is the twofold ignorance, coemergent ignorance and conceptual ignorance. If these two were purified, we would be buddhas. But as long as the coemergent and conceptual aspects of ignorance are not purified, we are sentient beings.

స

INDIVISIBLE

དབྱེར་མེད།

Do not divide appearances as being there and awareness as being here, let appearance and awareness be indivisible.

ঙ

INNATE

གཉུག་མ།

Innate means uninterrupted or natural; the original, natural state free from concepts.

ঙ

INTELLECTUAL UNDERSTANDING

གོ་བ།

The view that has strayed into intellectual under-standing is like a patch; it will wear off, fall apart. The patch is not the clothing itself. Intellectual under-standing is different from the view; it does not destroy dualistic fixation.

KARMAS

ལས།

Habitual patterns and deluded experience are actually the most detrimental. Unless we are able to destroy them right now, later, after death, it is not possible to do so, because our karmas and disturbing emotions are too powerful.

༄

Sentient beings fixate on thoughts; the true yogi does not. Sentient beings' thoughts are like carving in stone; whatever is thought stays, leaving a trace. Whatever the mental act, a trace remains. This is why we must accept that there is karma, there are disturbing emotions and there are habitual patterns. But, on the other hand, the thoughts occurring in the true yogi's mind are like drawings in air. There is an apparent movement, but it is only seeming because he perceives the nature of his mind. There is no dualistic clinging to perceiver and perceived and, hence, no karmic accumulation whatsoever. This is the meaning of unceasing, self-occurring self-liberation.

༄

It is not possible to be enlightened while still having obscurations and negative karma. They need to be interrupted and purified, and that is why one does the purification practices and apologizes for any negative deeds one has done. There is also a way to thoroughly and perpetually bring an end to negative karma and obscuration. The moment of recognizing mind essence totally interrupts the karma and obscurations, for that moment. It purifies the negative karma that has been continued from the past and it interrupts any creation henceforth. As long as this recognition lasts, karma and obscurations are thoroughly and completely ended. Complete stability in the recognition of the empty cognizance, therefore, involves the total elimination of all obscurations and negative karma.

ॐ

KNOWING, UNKNOWING
རིག་དང་མ་རིག

The ignorance of unknowing, grasping at duality, getting involved in the three poisons — these directly obscure the all-encompassing purity of what appears and exists. The difference between samsara and nirvana lies wholly between knowing and not knowing. When someone has recognized his or her nature by having it pointed out by a master, that is knowing what is to be as it is. This is what one then trains in — the state of original wakefulness unspoiled by dualistic fixation.

The dividing line between samsara and nirvana is between knowing and not knowing the self-cognizant, original wakefulness. When there is knowing, it is nirvana; when not knowing, it is samsara. What is it that is to be known? That our nature is the unity of empty cognizance, that the three kayas of the buddhas are not outside, but complete within the essence of mind — your *own* mind.

Recognizing and knowing this is nirvana. Not knowing how to recognize that the three kayas of buddhahood are present in oneself is unknowing, which is samsara.

LAMA

བླ་མ།

The Tibetan word for guru is *lama*. One explanation is that 'la' refers to the vital force of all sentient beings while 'ma' is the mother of all sentient beings. This demonstrates that it is the essence, as well as the source of all sentient beings. This is one explanation. Another is that 'la' means unexcelled, unsurpassable, nothing higher than that.

ॐ

Among the different kinds of gurus, the one who introduces the unborn Dharmakaya of your own mind is called the precious root guru.

ॐ

LETTING GO

ཆམ་མེར་བཞག་པ།

Letting go into mind essence does not mean that there is something that is being let go of and somebody who lets go. Letting go is without two, without duality.

LIBERATION FROM SAMSARA
འཁོར་བ་ལས་ཐར་བ།

The three higher realms are the realms of human beings, demigods, and gods. An even higher achievement is liberation from samsara, rebirth in one of the buddhafields. Higher than even liberation is buddhahood, complete enlightenment itself.

LIBERATION OF THOUGHTS AND EMOTIONS
ཉོན་རྟོག་གྲོལ་བ།

Liberation is only possible through realizing the basic unity of experience and emptiness.

When the expression of awareness moves as knowledge, there is liberation. When it moves as conceptual thoughts, there is confusion. In the essence itself, there is no waxing or waning. Both confusion and liberation occur in the expression.

While awareness itself is being recognized, thoughts are like a reflection appearing on the surface of a mirror. No matter what kind of image may appear: white, red, black, beautiful or ugly, the mirror is not harmed in any way whatsoever; nothing remains on it. Likewise, in the continuity of awareness, the vivid wakefulness, all that arises, any possible thoughts that might move are all the expression of awareness. One is able to understand that they are harmless, just like the play of children. This is confidence in liberation.

MEANINGFUL

དོན་དང་ལྡན་པ།

In this life, only the pursuance of buddhahood, the state of complete enlightenment is meaningful.

MEANS AND KNOWLEDGE

ཐབས་དང་ཤེས་རབ།

The potential for enlightenment is present as the nature of our own mind. To recognize this fact is the knowledge aspect. In order to fully facilitate this recognition we apply the means — visualizing the Buddha, making praises, and performing different types of conceptual practices.

The true path of the buddhas is the unity of means and knowledge. It is not sufficient to simply apply the means, thinking that a superior being is outside oneself and making offerings and praises to that external image. Only by combining the two aspects of means and knowledge do we attain enlightenment.

ॐ

If means and knowledge are separated it is difficult to attain buddhahood. If you think about it, actually it is impossible to complete a work, even in this samsaric world, without means and knowledge.

ॐ

The basis of the Mahayana is the two precious kinds of bodhichitta. According to the Sutra path one accomplishes enlightenment through emptiness and compassion. Emptiness is the path of knowledge (*prajña*) and compassion is the path of means (*upaya*). According to the Sutra system, the true root of means and knowledge is emptiness and compassion. According to Mantra, means is the development stage and knowledge is the completion stage; through the development and completion stages, one attains the unified level of Vajradhara. These are the special principles of Sutra and Mantra. The root of both kinds of precious bodhichitta, the relative and absolute, is complete within compassionate emptiness.

༄

MEDITATION, MEDITATOR
བསྒོམ་བྱ་སྒོམ་བྱེད།

In the training of recognizing the essence of empty cognizance there is not even as much as a hair tip to create or imagine as an act of meditating. We simply need to grow used to recognizing.

༄

For practice, it is said, the best looseness makes the best meditation, medium looseness makes medium meditation and the lowest looseness makes the lowest meditation.

༄

What brings us down is the idea of meditator and meditated, taking self-existing wakefulness as something to meditate on and one's conceptual mind as the meditator. One may have gained the intellectual understanding that there is an empty and cognizant state and holds it in mind: "Ah, the Lama said there was something empty and cognizant. Oh yes! This must be it. Now I must not lose it through distraction." In this case, the whole experience is a fabrication.

During all daily activities, whatever you are doing, whether there is thought occurrence or stillness, whether you feel anger, desire, happiness, or sadness, whether it is past, future or right now — at all times — there is merely something to recognize, not something to meditate on. Stillness or movement of attention are like a person sitting and moving about. Whether you move around or not, you should still recognize your own face.

MINDFULNESS

དྲན་ཤེས།

We begin with mindfulness in order to find our way out of the delusion and dualistic fixation that have gone on endlessly in samsara. Mindfulness, however, could have a definite dualistic connotation. It could be like putting a hook in a piece of meat and holding it steady so that a dog does not run off with it. There is a subject keeping an eye on the object. There is a more subtle level called watchfulness, which is a mere noticing, but it also is subtly dualistic. Even subtler than watchfulness is awakeness. That is the point of separating *sem* and rigpa. Sem, the dualistic frame of mind, means involvement with thoughts of either past, present or future. Rigpa simply means the awakened state that is uninvolved in thoughts of the three times.

Honestly, for a beginner, without the mindfulness of reminding, there is no recognition of mind essence. That is called deliberate mindfulness. It is dualistic mind that reminds you to recognize, but the seeing of no thing to be seen is rigpa, the awakened state free of duality.

93

The method for nondistraction is mindfulness.

୭

Although dharmakaya permeates all of samsara and nirvana, whatever appears and exists, if we do not recognize we continue in this wild habit we have fallen into since beginningless time up until now. That is why it is necessary to apply mindfulness.

୭

Due to the power of having become acquainted with the free resting of not meditating on something 'there', one will remain awake in awareness and at that point watcher and watched are mingled and fall away. But until then one needs to apply mindfulness.

୭

According to the Dzogchen system, first there is deliberate mindfulness, literally the mindfulness of deliberate attention. You should exert yourself in this and once you have become quite accustomed to it, you will, at some stage, automatically get into effortless mindfulness, where there is no need to push. As soon as one is carried away, one notices, "I am distracted," and immediately you arrive back in awareness.

To keep an eye on whether one is distracted or not, first of all, one needs effortful mindfulness. When that slowly, slowly has become habituated it becomes effortless. By effortful mindfulness, one is led to the effortless.

৵

When effortful mindfulness has become self-sustained, there is a vivid, wakeful, effortless state of being awake without any need for force or struggle, without any rigidity, just naturally alert. When you become accustomed, there is only undistracted rigpa.

৵

It is said, "Sustain primordially free awareness with natural mindfulness." That means without being distracted, without being carried away, exactly as it is, rest freely. Although this self-abiding nondistraction is called mindfulness, in this context there is no duality.

৵

Initially we do need to meditate with some effort to approach the state of effortlessness. It is said, "The path of effort leads to effortlessness." In the Middle Way, this deliberate effort to meditate is called mindfulness.

Mindfulness is attentive, in that there is a sense of being alert and careful. To be both mindful and attentive is to be conscientious. Finally, the mindfulness becomes free from the four limits and eight constructs. According to Mahamudra, this effort is called watchfulness. Watchfulness is like a herdsman who keeps his eye on the cattle and pays attention to whether they drink water or eat grass. Emphasizing watchfulness entails noticing how the mind is. You need somebody to keep watch on that. In the Dzogchen tradition it is called awakeness, in which mindfulness and awareness are indivisible. Mindfulness and rigpa-awareness are not two different things.

To sustain primordially free awareness with natural mindfulness is to be without an atom upon which to meditate and without slipping into distraction for even an instant. That is called being mindful in the state of undistracted nonmeditation. You should be mindful in the state of not being distracted while not meditating. By being mindful in this way, you do not get distracted nor do you artificially meditate upon anything. Meditating is conceptual mind; being distracted is to stray into confusion.

෴

In Dzogchen, mindfulness is rigpa; rigpa is mind-fulness.

෴

MISDEEDS
སྡིག་པ།

Misdeeds, or evil actions, refer to unwholesome, negative, evil behavior, like stealing, lying, or taking another's life. Misdeeds create negative karma, and being involved in such actions *does* prevent the realization of buddha nature.

෴

MOMENTARY
བློ་བུར་བ།

The momentary occurrence of thoughts and fixation prevents full realization of our innate nature of self-existing wakefulness. However, because this occurrence is momentary, it can be cleared away.

೨

If we are traveling toward Bodhgaya, an analogy for enlightenment, unless we fly by air, there are mountains, rivers and valleys, ups and downs; there are comfortable places and steep places, all different kinds. Likewise, self-existing wakefulness is bound within this body made of aggregates and elements. Due to the functions of the five elements and the nadis and winds, sometimes we feel at ease, sometimes disturbed, sometimes, even without an external cause, the mind can become irritated. Without any external painful objects, we can suffer and although there is no suffering or pain in the enlightened essence itself, because it is tied down within momentary habitual patterns, we experience all kinds of things while in the body. But as long as we are headed for Bodhgaya, whether there are ups or downs, hills or valleys, if we do not stop anywhere, eventually we will arrive at our destination.

೨

MOTIVATION

All Dharmas depend on our motivation. There are two kinds, that of Mahayana and that of Vajrayana. These are called 'the vast and the profound' respectively. The Sutra aspect is to be motivated by compassion: to consider that all sentient beings in the three realms of samsara have, without a single exception, been our parents, the distance in time being their only difference from our present parents. The Vajrayana motivation is to consider that the outer universe is a celestial palace and that its 'inner contents', sentient beings, have the nature of male and female deities — there is no impurity whatsoever. Whether or not the Dharma carries you forward on a perfect path depends on your motivation. So, first bring forth the Sutra and Mantra motivation and then proceed with your practice.

৺

NATURALNESS

རང་བབས།

Let be in naturalness. While seeing your essence — seeing that there is no thing to see — the training is simply to let be in naturalness. Naturalness means without technique, without artifice.

ॐ

Unfabricated naturalness means you do not have to do anything during that state. It is like ringing a bell. Once you ring the bell, there is a continuity of sound; you do not have to do anything in order for the sound to continue.

ॐ

We do not need to *make* this unfabricated naturalness. Simply give up thinking of the three times.

ॐ

This is a training in *not* meditating, a training in naturalness, in letting be.

ॐ

NONDISTRACTION

ག་ཡེང་མེད།

The main part of meditation practice it to remain without distraction.

৽

Contrived nondistraction is to merely sit and hold the idea of being undistracted. A certain Tibetan medicine against stomach disorder, if not digested, can turn poisonous in the stomach. This is like the idea of sitting and thinking, "I am not distracted, I am not distracted." It is simply a thought.

৽

NONMEDITATION

སྒོམ་མེད།

Nonmeditation means not contriving, not imagining. Nondistraction means not forgetting. Steadiness or continuity comes from not being distracted, and this is not something that we have to push or force ourselves to do, because it is also nonmeditation. There is no *doing*, in the sense of deliberate meditation taking place. This is the essential point: undistracted non-meditation. Train in that. If you keep at it, at a certain point your training becomes like the steady, unbroken flow of a river.

To express one hundred essential points with one sentence: it is undistracted nonmeditation. This means to not slip into distraction for even an instant while not meditating on even a dust mote. Once we become distracted, the continuity is lost.

OBSCURATIONS

Dribpa, means obscuration, veil, or cover. Dribpa can be compared to the walls of this room: they prevent us from seeing what is going on outside; our vision is obstructed. These obscurations are something subtler that prevents us from realizing the nature as it is.

The state of buddhahood is within us. The essence is primordially enlightened, but temporarily obscured. The veils can be cleared away.

There are various methods for clearing away these temporary obscurations. The long path involves training in being virtuous in the ten ways. The shorter route is the Vajrayana training in deity, mantra and samadhi. The fastest route is to exert yourself in realizing the wish-fulfilling jewel of the nature of mind, and recognizing mind essence itself. Because what obscures buddha nature is something temporary, exert yourself in removing these obscurations.

༄

OBSTACLES

བར་ཆད།

The outer obstacles are disturbances of the outer elements, the inner obstacles are disturbances of the nadis and pranas, and the innermost obstacles are dualistic clinging to perceiver and perceived. Basically, the latter refers to our habit of dualistic experience, which is caused by a lack of stability in the original basic state of empty cognizance.

Whatever sickness or unhappiness you have, the greater the difficulty the better the opportunity for practice. When you feel deeply distressed and troubled that is the perfect time to practice meditation. Most people cannot practice when they are happy and joyful. When they are depressed, sick and suffer, the real remedy is meditation practice.

To think, "First, I will get all favorable conditions together and then practice the Dharma," is to be possessed by Mara before even starting Dharma practice. That is the demon of the son of the gods. If you practice immediately, whether conditions are good or bad, obstacles will gradually fall away by themselves.

Every level of teaching has its own purpose. Although the very heart of the Buddhadharma is to recognize mind essence and train in that, still, there are obstacles and hindrances that need to be cleared away and enhancement practices that need to be done. An obstacle prevents us from remaining in the natural state. These can be cleared away by certain practices.

OBSTRUCTERS

བགེགས།

Understand that obstructing forces are your own thoughts, they arise out of your own mind. The basic hindrance or obstructer is the tendency to conceptualize a subject and object duality. The word obstructer means that which creates a hindrance to realization of the enlightened state.

Obstructing forces are one's own thoughts arising externally; they are also called harmful spirits. They are the forces that pull one back from attaining the state of enlightenment and they originate from one's own thoughts, from ignorance.

"The obstructers are going to harm me!" There is duality when thinking "I and that." "The demons are there and I am here!" That is dualistic fixation.

OPENNESS

ཟང་ཐལ།

Complete openness, *zangtal* in Tibetan, means not attached to anything, not fixating on anything. This is precisely the opposite of an ordinary person's frame of mind clinging to and fixating on everything. The openness of rigpa, the openness of a yogi, does not fixate on anything; it does not hold on to anything. We need to grow used to this type of openness. Let your five senses be wide open, wide awake and yet thought-free. Remain in that state, utterly open.

༄

Nondual awareness is primordially open, free. This openness means naturally free. However, this openness becomes bound by the rope of conceptual mind when a sentient being is fettered by conceptual thoughts in a body of karmic ripening. It seemingly loses its natural freedom.

༄

The awakened state of rigpa is wide open. Nothing is fixated upon or held onto, like the ocean in which no sediment remains.

ORDINARY MIND

ཐ་མལ་གྱི་ཤེས་པ།

There is no need to do anything to your present wakefulness at the moment of recognizing; it is already as it is. That is the true meaning of naked ordinary mind, a famous term in Tibetan, *tamal kyi shepa*. It means not tampered with. There is no 'thing' which needs to be accepted or rejected; it is simply as it is. The term 'ordinary mind' is the most immediate and accurate term to describe the nature of mind. No matter what terminology is being utilized within the Middle Way, Mahamudra or Dzogchen, naked ordinary mind is the simplest term.

The present moment of unfabricated wakefulness is seen the moment we look. Sometimes it is called present mind, ordinary mind or naked mind. Ordinary mind means that it is neither worsened nor improved. Ordinary means that unceasing wakefulness is present in all beings from Samantabhadra down to the tiniest insect. This unceasing wakefulness is the true Samantabhadra.

PATH

ལམ།

Right now among the ground, path and fruition we are at the path stage. At the stage of the path, we cannot have the view of the fruition. If the obscurations are not purified and the accumulations not gathered you will not be able to realize the true meaning of self-existing wakefulness. Therefore, you should first purify the obscurations and gather the accumulations.

๛

Actually, awareness itself is without anything to be cultivated. There is something to recognize, for without recognizing you are simply a sentient being. You need to recognize primordially free awareness. This is the actual beginning, the taking hold of the true path of enlightenment. Primordially free awareness is present within the mind-stream of all sentient beings. They do not recognize it, but practitioners do.

๛

Appearances of form are the nature of the deities' body. All sounds are the nature of the deities' speech.

All thoughts are the nature of the deities' mind. These acknowledgements are the three things to carry concerning sights, sounds and awareness. To carry means to bring onto the path, it means not to abandon.

ॐ

Buddhahood, the realized state of all awakened beings, does not stray back to the path of confusion due to having recognized the state of the ground as being pure gold. Our pure gold, on the other hand, is temporarily covered by mud due to the power of confusion; we have strayed onto the state of the path. We are now temporarily under the power of confusion.

ॐ

PERSEVERANCE
བརྩོན་འགྲུས།

Perseverance, in the context of recognizing mind essence, should be like the unbroken flow of a river. Is there ever any second when the Ganges does not flow? It is a steady, unbroken current. Nobody is pushing or pulling it down the riverbed. It simply flows. Of course, there may be a difference in volume or intensity as to how much water is passing through, but the basic flow of the river is never ever interrupted. Another example is the constancy of a taut bowstring. Once you bend the bow and make the string taut, it does not sometimes become tighter and sometimes slack. It stays at an even tension. We should have this kind of perseverance: steady, so that we do not alternate between sometimes struggling and pushing ourselves hard while at other times totally giving up.

How is it possible to exert oneself without fluctuation? By training in undistracted nonmeditation.

ॐ

PHENOMENA

ཆོས་དང་སྣང་བ།

Phenomena manifest in both pure and impure forms. Impure phenomena are the mundane experiences in this world. Pure phenomena are when there is no dualistic clinging. After becoming accustomed to the indivisible, unconfined, and undeluded state of dharmakaya, all phenomena appear without any self-nature.

ॐ

Confused thinking fools us and prevents us from pure perception. Impure phenomena are thus the manifestation of our own deluded thinking. Impure phenomena — the unaware ways of perception — are the same as dream phenomena. Once we wake up from the delusion of sleep, they disappear.

The moment of recognizing mind essence is the instant that impure experience, the habit of fixating on all things as solid reality, disperses into basic space. What is left is pure experience, pure phenomena.

POINTING-OUT INSTRUCTION

The pointing-out instruction is the method through which one is introduced to and is able to recognize the nature of this mind, the buddha nature.

The pointing-out instruction is your present wakefulness pointed out as it is.

The first thing we are introduced to in Dzogchen is the state of nonmeditation — insight free of concepts, free of the watcher and something watched.

PRECIOUS WORD EMPOWERMENT

ཚིག་དབང་རིན་པོ་ཆེ།

The precious word empowerment cuts through the flow of conceptual thinking to introduce empty cognizance, the innate state of original mind. It was never really concealed; it is only seemingly concealed from sentient beings because their attention is occupied with other things. When that is the case, you may hear about the nature of mind, but it feels hidden from you; it is not an actuality. The moment one recognizes mind nature it is seen immediately, and it is no longer hidden or far away. It has been brought into actual experience, which is exactly the point of the fourth empowerment.

PRELIMINARIES

སྔོན་འགྲོ།

If you want to practice many extensive details, you can find hundreds of thousands of teachings in the Buddhist canonical collection, but it is impossible to practice them all in a single lifetime. Padmasambhava and other masters kindly extracted the essence of the teachings in developing the preliminary practices, which include all the instructions of the scholars and accomplished beings of India and Tibet.

Some people may think that the preliminary practices are somehow inferior and that the following main part is deeper and more important. That is not so. As it is said in the oral lineage, "Compared to the main part, the preliminaries are more profound." For instance, when we build a house, if the foundation is firm, we can easily construct many hundreds of stories on top. Without a stable basis, the whole house, however tall it may be, will never be stable.

For all Dharma practice, one should first lay a firm foundation with the preliminaries. On this foundation, it is then possible to build the progressively higher 'stories' of the main part.

℘

Honestly, if one has received the teachings on mind essence and practices the preliminaries while remembering to recognize nature of mind, it multiplies their effect tremendously. It is taught that to practice with a pure attitude multiplies the effect one hundred times, while to practice with pure samadhi multiplies the effect one hundred thousand times. Combine the preliminaries with the recognition of mind essence and your practice will be tremendously effective.

℘

PRIMORDIAL PURITY

ཀ་དག

When we attain stability in primordial purity, we take control of our own territory. When we have re-assumed primordial purity, we can manifest as the sambhogakaya buddha of rainbow-colored light.

VAJRA SPEECH

All the phenomena of appearance and existence, perceiver and perceived, do not possess even a hair tip of concrete existence. Primordial purity does not have any concreteness. All the phenomena of samsara and nirvana appear from the space of primordial purity.

PROTECTORS

ཆོས་སྐྱོང་།

Sometimes it is not even necessary to invoke the protectors of the Dharma. There are both those you have to and those you do not have to enjoin. If one has great realization, the protectors will be scrambling to help you. Lacking realization, there is no certainty it will help no matter how long you enjoin them.

ॐ

PURE PERCEPTION

དག་སྣང་།

Sacred outlook, pure perception, is the special quality of Vajrayana. Sacred outlook refers to seeing things as they actually are, not in the ordinary deluded way of regarding earth as simply solid matter and water as merely water, wind as wind, etc. In actuality, the five elements are the five female buddhas; the five aggregates are the five male buddhas, and so forth. Therefore, training in pure perception is not a way of convincing oneself that things are what they are not, but rather training in seeing things as they truly are.

Actually, Vajrayana is nothing other than pure perception from the very beginning. One should never be apart from pure perception. The outer world is pure, all sentient beings are dakas and dakinis. Even dogs and pigs, although they appear to be impure beings, still possess the enlightened essence. They also possess the properties of flesh, blood, warmth and breath. They possess the five elements and five aggregates which are of the nature of the five male and five female buddhas.

It is merely that our immediate way of perceiving is not pure, but when we have become a true yogi, everything is seen as purity within our own perception. Ordinary sentient beings do not see that way because they cannot perceive the purity. This is the difference between personal perception and others' perception. One *can* see other beings as pure because they are already pure.

༄

For a true yogi, everything, within and without, has the purity of body, speech, mind, qualities and activities. In a yogi's perception, there is not even a dust mote of impurity. This is called the great equality of samsara and nirvana. The yogi sees samsara and nirvana as great equality, because they are like that. Although it might not appear like this to others, when obscurations and habitual patterns are purified everything is seen as pure in one's own perception.

༄

The worldly experience of phenomena is called impure perception. Impure perception is the confused perception of sentient beings. For someone who only has pure perceptions, a house will be experienced as a celestial palace. In the celestial palace, there is no experience of earth, water, fire and wind. Everything is rainbow light, major and minor bindus. How amazing that would be!

Buddha Samantabhadra is like a foundation. Samantabhadra is not only the foundation for the pure but also for the impure. In actuality, there is not even a sesame seed of impurity. It is one's own perceptions that are deluded and nothing else.

QUALIFIED TEACHER

མཆོན་ལྡན་བླ་མ།

The foremost qualified teacher is a 'vajra-holder possessing the three precepts'. He or she should possess the perfect qualities of being outwardly endowed with the vows of individual liberation, the *pratimoksha*, while inwardly possessing the trainings of a bodhisattva. On the innermost level, the qualified master must be competent in the true state of samadhi.

A person who possesses only the vows of individual liberation that correspond to Hinayana practice, is known as a 'virtuous guide'. If a person also possesses the bodhisattva trainings, he or she is called a 'spiritual teacher'. If a person is adept in the Vajrayana practices along with these vows and trainings, he or she is recognized as a *dorje lobpön*, a vajra master.

A true vajra master should have already liberated his own stream-of-being through realization. This means actualizing the authentic state of samadhi. Furthermore, he or she should be able to liberate others through compassion and loving kindness.

QUALITIES

ཡོན་ཏན།

It is said that first nonexistence is explained, then existence, and finally the union of existence and nonexistence. In the context of mind essence, nonexistence elucidates its primordial purity while existence concerns its spontaneously present nature. The indivisibility of existence and nonexistence describes that primordial purity and spontaneous presence are a unity. These are the qualities of rigpa. All enlightened qualities are qualities of rigpa.

REALIZATION

It is said, "When misdeeds are purified, realization occurs automatically." When your intrinsic buddha nature is free from any veil, it is naturally stable in itself. But normally it is obscured by unwholesome tendencies. Don't the clouds covering the sky make it impossible to clearly see the stars and planets?

Realization in this sense means that the stream of conceptual thinking becomes self-arising self-liberation until your state of mind is finally like a clear, cloudless sky. At that point, since there is no more distraction, conceptual thinking has naturally dissolved.

RECITATION

བཟླས་པ།

Recitation has three aspects: approach, accomplishment and activity. The meaning of approach is like first approaching the king by making a petition — you write a letter asking to be granted such and such powers or permission. Accomplishment is when you actually get the permission to do what you want — the king kindly bestows a favor upon you and you obtain some authority. So, approach means to beseech and accomplishment to take charge. After that, you can carry out whatever activity you find necessary: increasing, pacifying, magnetizing or subjugating. To re-iterate, first one petitions the king for a certain mandate, then one receives the authority. After that, one uses this authority to carry out activities by sending out emissaries to do the job. The king himself does not go and carry out his activities, he sends his emissaries, his ministers, police, etc.

༈

RECOGNIZE

ངོ་ཤེས་པ།

The word 'recognize' literally means meeting your nature head-on, to recognize your own essence face-to-face. It means acknowledging what you already have, not something newly produced from elsewhere.

That which knows is empty in essence, cognizant by nature, and its capacity is unconfined. Try to see this for yourself and understand that this is how your essence is. Thoughts arise from you and dissolve into you; they do not arise and dissolve somewhere else. If you recognize the source of thoughts, they dissolve into your own empty cognizance.

So, what is recognized, when we say 'recognize'? It means seeing that the nature of mind is an unconfined empty cognizance. This is the real condition, the natural state of the three kayas.

ॐ

Delusion seemingly separates sentient beings from buddha nature. Eventually, when the delusion is cleared up, it is this very buddha nature that clears up the delusion. The hundred sublime peaceful and wrathful buddhas, including Buddha Samantabhadra, were never deluded. When failing to recognize, one is deluded. But delusion dissolves the very moment you recognize the identity of that which is deluded.

ॐ

Dualistic mind's activity of thinking arises as the expression of unrecognized awareness. Once you recognize basic awareness, the display of thoughts loses all power and simply dissolves into the expanse of buddha nature. This is the basic reason to recognize mind essence.

ॐ

What we recognize and train in should, from the very beginning, have the same identity as that of complete enlightenment. We should recognize and train in the state of nonmeditation as the path.

ॐ

Actually, nondual awareness is without something to be cultivated or meditated upon. There is something to recognize, for without recognizing you are simply a sentient being. The actual beginning of the path is to recognize the primordially free awareness that is present within the mind-stream of all sentient beings. They fail to recognize it, but practitioners do recognize it. What it comes down to is whether or not it is recognized.

ॐ

Saraha said, "Give up the thinker and what is thought of." That is the actual way of benefiting beings. But giving up everything does not include giving up recognizing. Give up doing, but do not give up nondoing. If you give up recognizing, you remain in a state of indifference. Give up conceptual experience, but do not give up nonconceptual wakefulness.

RELATIVE AND ABSOLUTE
ཀུན་རྫོབ་དང་དོན་དམ།

While conventional truth means the conceptual frame of mind, ultimate truth means the reality of the true meaning. It is also called transcendent knowledge, *prajnaparamita*. In Dzogchen it is known as the immaculate dharmakaya of empty awareness.

The real condition of things is as they actually are, not just how they seem. The seeming way is created by our normal rigid and fixating thoughts. Recognize the real state and the seeming way vanishes. These are the two aspects: the real and the seeming, the ultimate and the relative. The real is your essence; the seeming is your thoughts. Once you recognize the real state, the seeming way collapses, dissolves and vanishes without a trace. That is what this training is all about.

৽

The Sutra system talks about the relative and ultimate truth. The Great Perfection teaches the way it appears and the way it is, the seeming and the real. For instance, the real is the present condition of the deities within one's body. The seeming is when the external world is visualized as a celestial palace within which one visualizes the hundred sublime peaceful and wrathful buddhas.

৽

RENUNCIATION
ངེས་འབྱུང་།

Renunciation is the true sign of accomplishment, blessing and realization. Renunciation means to understand that time is running out and everything passes. In other words, it is a natural disenchantment with samsaric attainments and any samsaric state.

৽

REPEATING MANY TIMES

གྲངས་མང་།

The only way to acquire all the great qualities of enlightenment is to repeat many times the short moment of recognizing mind essence. There is no other method. One reason for short moments is that, as there is no stability right now, the recognition of awareness doesn't last for more than a brief moment, whether we like it or not. By practicing many times, we get used to it.

ॐ

The virtue of repeating short periods many times is that it is unspoiled by conceptual mind. If it lasts a long time, it is influenced by concepts. If we remain for a long time, it is only our intellect prolonging it. This state should endure by itself, automatically. If it is not natural but contrived, it will be spoiled. Therefore, in repeating a short period many times, that short period will be automatic or natural.

ॐ

RETREAT

མཚམས།

A quiet place is considered extremely important. This is because in such a place, all hustle, bustle and mental constructs cease and you automatically arrive at simplicity.

ৡ

Honestly, there is hardly as much as one instant during a twenty-four hour period when an ordinary person truly remains in uncontrived naturalness. This habit is the exact opposite of Dharma practice. We need to train in the habit of samadhi. In the beginning, it seems very difficult. Unless we give up our normal tasks and distance ourselves from them, we have no opportunity to change our mind's deep-rooted negative habits. It simply will not happen. This is why all the buddhas and great masters encouraged people to seek out quiet places to grow stable in the recognition of their buddha nature. The Mahamudra tradition tells us that by practicing the threefold solitude one grows closer to and realizes the innate three vajras. The Dzogchen tradition tells us to abandon the ninefold activities. This profound and amazing instruction is not easy to do while involved in ordinary life. That is the reason why all the great masters encouraged practitioners to stay in retreat.

The main result of solitude is that pointless activities naturally diminish. There is a famous statement, "By abandoning activities, you approach the nature of nondoing." That is the entire reason for staying in mountain retreats. Otherwise, without meditation practice what would be the reason for staying in a cave? A cave is not necessary to build. Some people miss the point and spend time interior decorating and making cave improvements. They end up owning the cave, thinking, "What a great place to live." They forget the quote about nondoing.

All the texts say that one should begin retreat by offering a feast. One should also give a torma to the deity of the locality. Then one offers the feast to the Three Roots to not have obstacles and to swiftly accomplish the supreme and common siddhis.

In solitude is where all the gurus attained enlightenment within one life and body. They never stayed where their body, speech and mind were not in solitude. This is an important point. When the body is in solitude then one attains the vajra body, when the speech is in solitude one attains the vajra speech, and when the mind is in solitude one attains the vajra mind. The three vajras are attained by remaining in mountain solitude.

REVULSION

ཞེན་ལོག

Revulsion is losing our appetite for samsaric existence and realizing that samsaric pursuits are futile and do not yield any permanent pleasure or happiness whatsoever.

Revulsion is like the feeling people suffering from jaundice experience when served fried food; they either get very nauseous or they vomit. In the same way, when we realize that all the achievements of the six realms of samsara are futile, insubstantial and meaningless, we lose our appetite for them.

RIGPA

རིག་པ།

In the case of stillness, occurrence and noticing, the word rigpa is used for noticing. Self-existing awareness is also called rigpa. The word is the same but the meaning is different. The difference between these two practices is as vast as the distance between sky and earth. In the case of stillness, occurrence and noticing, rigpa means observing and being aware of whether the mind is still or whether there is thought occurrence. Self-existing awareness, on the other hand, transcends both thinking and being still.

Dualistic mind is self-abandoned the moment awareness is recognized. Distinguish between these two because dualistic mind changes while awareness does not. It is like the example of the sky being unchanging and the clouds changeable.

Samantabhadra is not a person who appeared sometime in the ancient past. Samantabhadra is rigpa itself since rigpa is the undeluded dharmakaya the moment it is recognized.

ം

As space pervades, awareness pervades. Like space, rigpa is all-encompassing, nothing is outside of it. Just as the world and beings are all pervaded by space, rigpa pervades the minds of all beings.

ം

No one is without rigpa. It is only that it is not recognized. Rigpa is nonconceptual, free from conceptual thought, yet it is cognizant. Without cognizance, one could not know anything.

ം

Unbound, free, naked, fresh — rigpa is not something that we need to make. This is where we all must arrive.

ം

Being flawless and endowed with all the perfect qualities, you cannot criticize rigpa even if you wanted to. Being indescribable, you cannot find a word, concept, or analogy — it transcends conceptual knowledge. In other words, even scientists cannot figure it out. Scientists always understand what they can grasp, but transcendent knowledge means what lies beyond the intellect's grasp. It is not formed in any way; it does not arise or come into being; it is like the essence of space. Yet, it is within the domain of our individual experience. We can experience it. You cannot recognize someone else's mind but you can know your own mind. It is right here; it is not some other place. In other words, it is the domain of self-cognizant wakefulness. This self-cognizant wakefulness is within our reach. You *can* know it.

ॐ

SADHANA

སྒྲུབ་ཐབས།

In Vajrayana, sadhana practice is the act of manifesting what is originally present in the form of the threefold mandalas of deity, mantra and samadhi.

ॐ

The purpose of sadhana is to enable blessings to enter our being and bless our mind-stream. The ritual is not to please the deities and fill their stomachs with offerings. It is for us to clear away our negative karma, purify our obscurations and attain the two kinds of accomplishments. The correct seeing of mind essence depends upon this purity.

Whether you can remain in the natural state or not depends on your merit. If you know how to recognize awareness, it is good to do so. If you do not know nor do any sadhana practice, you are doing nothing at all. You are merely eating through your mouth and shitting through your ass like a dog or pig.

Out of the expanse of the three kayas, the practice of sadhana takes place for the benefit of beings. You may have been introduced to the nature of mind and recognized the samadhi of suchness. Suchness means how our basic nature really is, not merely how one imagines it to be. While not departing from this state of suchness — while recognizing mind essence — one can then allow the different aspects of development stage to be played out or displayed, without leaving the state of suchness behind. That is the real unity of development and completion. There is a real way and a simulated way, and without recognizing mind essence there is no chance that one can practice the real way.

The perspective of Ati Yoga is contained within the sadhana text, and the sadhana text is embodied in one's personal application. To use a sadhana text in one's personal practice accumulates immense merit and purifies a vast amount of obscurations. That is a great fortune. The sadhana embodies the tantras of Mahayoga, the scriptures of Anu Yoga and the instructions of Ati Yoga.

In the context of sadhana, we should allow our nature to be as it is. In actuality, our nature is no different from the nature of all the buddhas. Simply read the sadhana's lines while leaving your mind in its natural state and the three samadhis naturally occur. For instance, simply think, "I am the deity Vajrasattva, my speech is Vajrasattva's mantra and my mind is indivisible from Vajrasattva." Remain like that in uncontrived naturalness.

ॐ

SAMADHI

ཏིང་ངེ་འཛིན།

Only the authentic state of samadhi can clear up our self-created confusion. More appearances and further fixating will not destroy our confusion.

ॐ

Stability in samadhi dismantles the entire show of delusion. Our mind created delusion, but by recognizing the nature of this mind, we clear it up, since at that moment no delusion can be re-created.

ॐ

SAMANTABHADRA & SAMANTABHADRI

ཀུན་བཟང་ཡབ་ཡུམ།

Our old father is called dharmakaya Samantabhadra and our old mother is dharmakaya Samantabhadri. All buddhas and sentient beings of the six realms are the offspring of this couple, who are not real entities, but unconfined empty cognizance. The empty quality is Samantabhadri, the great dharmakaya mother, who is also known as Vajra Varahi or Jetsün Tara. The cognizant quality is the dharmakaya Buddha Samantabhadra, also known as Vajradhara or Vajrasattva, our old dad.

The ultimate Dharma is the realization that basic space and awareness are indivisible. That is the starting point and is pointed-out at the beginning. It is essential to understand this; otherwise, we might have the feeling that Samantabhadra and his consort are an old blue man and his old lady who lived aeons ago. It is not like that at all; Samantabhadra and his consort are the indivisible unity of basic space and awareness.

SAMAYA

དམ་ཚིག

The scriptures tell us to not associate with people who have the defect of broken samayas; we should not even drink the water in the same area. If the samayas are transgressed there is some flaw that is contagious. It will disturb your concentration and make your body sick.

ও

In the general classifications of samaya, you find the four stages called infraction, transgression, violation, and breach (literally: contradicting, damaging, breaking, and passing). These categories depend in part on the length of time that has passed since the samaya was damaged. After three years of still not having apologized, there is no longer any chance to mend the samaya. At this point it is overstepped and is considered beyond repair.

ও

Most important is the samaya with the guru; next is that with one's vajra brothers and sisters. Everyone, both master and disciples must keep the samayas. When this is done correctly and purely, the outcome is extremely profound. There is a saying among the masters of the past, "There is no enemy worse than a samaya violator; there is no companionship better than my guru." The real enemy is the breaking of samaya; it can damage the master's health and life. The breach of samaya among close or distant vajra brothers and sisters also creates negative karma and misfortune.

౿

The 'samaya' principle entails many details involving the hundred thousand sections of samaya precepts and so on. All of these can be condensed into the basics, the samayas of body, speech and mind. The samaya of body means to visualize the yidam deity, remembering that one's own form is the divine form of the yidam. The samaya of speech is to remember to chant mantra and the samaya of mind is to recognize mind essence. Those are the three basic principles of Vajrayana, known as deity, mantra and samadhi.

౿

Concerning samaya with the guru, do not hurt his physical form. Do not beat him or physically injure him in any way. To not break his command means to obey if he asks you to do something. In regards to the guru's mind, do not do anything that makes him upset or displeased. In addition to keeping the samaya with the guru's body, speech and mind, one also has to keep the samayas with one's own body, speech and mind as deity, mantra and samadhi. This twofold set of samayas of body, speech and mind, with the guru and oneself, includes all other samayas.

ॐ

The best way of keeping pure samaya is to not depart from the view. This is known as the 'nonkeeping great keeping of samaya'. That is what is meant by 'no thing to keep'. All the samayas of body, speech and mind are contained in constantly remaining in the practice of recognizing mind essence.

The next best is to keep the samayas of body, speech and mind. The samaya of body is to practice the development stage of the deity. The samaya of speech is the utterance of its mantra. And the samaya of mind is to meditate on compassion and emptiness, practicing the unity of development and completion stages.

The samaya of body is not to disturb or cause inconvenience to the guru's body. The samaya of speech is not to break his command or order. And the samaya of mind is to remain in the state of thinking his mind and one's own mind to be inseparable. These were the lowest samayas. (*Rinpoche laughs.*) The best is to remain in the practice.

৯

While we are caught up in dualistic mind, there are definitely samayas to keep and samayas that can be broken. But the moment conceptual mind dissolves into the expanse of nondual awareness; there is no samsara to be rejected and no nirvana to be accomplished. At that moment, you transcend the concepts of keeping and breaking. Until that point, however, there definitely are samayas to keep.

৯

The samayas for the Dzogchen teachings have two aspects: primordial purity and spontaneous presence — *kadag* and *lhündrub*. Primordial purity refers to the view of Trekchö, the 'thorough cut'. Spontaneous presence refers to the meditation training called Tögal. Each of these has two samayas. The samayas for Trekchö practice are called nonexistence and all-pervasiveness. The two samayas for Tögal training are oneness and spontaneous perfection. So, there are four samayas, nonexistence, all-pervasiveness, oneness and spontaneous perfection. Because everything is included within these four, these are known as the king-like samayas.

৯

Ultimately, to be totally free from any defects in your vows and samayas, you need to remain in the continuity of the four samayas of the Dzogchen view — nonexistence, all-pervasiveness, oneness and spontaneous perfection. If you are able to fulfill these, you totally transcend any possible violation or breach of samaya. To accomplish this you need to be able to dissolve dualistic mind in nondual awareness.

In short, the best way to keep the samayas intact is through the proper view, meditation and conduct. If that is not completely possible, patience is a strong basis for keeping samayas. It is said, "Do not retaliate with anger when attacked with rage. Do not retaliate with abuse when reviled. Do not retaliate with criticism when blamed in public. Do not retaliate with blows when threatened with physical violence." Be patient even if someone actually hits you. If you can be forbearing in this way, you will triumph over the enemy of broken samayas.

SAMSARA
འཁོར་བ།

Thought is the root and creator of samsara.

༄

Samsara, in general, has no end; but there is an end for each individual sentient being. There are always some beings who have not attained enlightenment, so there is no end to samsara. But at some time, there is an end for each individual. Therefore, it is said that there is no beginning, but if one practices there is an end.

༄

The state of being a buddha is undeluded like the sun shining in the cloudless sky. The state of mind of sentient beings is like the reflection of the sun on water. Just as the reflection is dependent upon water, our thoughts are dependent upon objects. The object is what is thought of, the subject is the perceiving mind. This clinging to perceiver and perceived is the cause for continuing in deluded samsaric existence, day and night, life after life.

༄

The only way to clear up the problem of samsaric existence is to dissolve ignorance into the primordial ground. This is done by simply recognizing the natural state of mind and not perpetuating the habit of dualistic clinging; simply let be in naturalness, without accepting or rejecting.

There is only one way to be perpetually free of the three poisons and end samsara: to grow fully trained in the recognition of mind essence, so that there is no longer any break in the seeing of the indivisible empty cognizance — so it is unbroken throughout day and night.

SESSIONS AND BREAKS
ཐུན་དང་ཐུན་མཚམས།

The Sutra teachings say that one should train in a meditation state that is like space and see the post-meditation like a magical illusion. But in Dzogchen, both the meditation and postmeditation should be like space free of constructs. Thinking that phenomena are like illusion is a mental fabrication.

ॐ

If you want to mingle this practice with daily life, do not differentiate between sessions and breaks. Breaks or postmeditation means to be distracted, to get carried away from the natural state by the power of distraction, like attaching reality to the eight examples of illusion.

ॐ

No division between sessions and breaks means not to lose the view during daily activities. Suppose you are able to remain in the view during the session but not during the breaks. In the breaks, you completely forget and lose the recognition of the essence. That is not good enough. Maintain the practice during both sessions and breaks.

ॐ

To practice nondistraction is the actual path without division between sessions and breaks.

ॐ

The best type of diligence is to never be separated from the practice. Whether it is a session or whether you are walking around, eating, sitting down, talking to people, remain in nondual awareness. If you practice like that, you will quickly attain stability and enlightenment.

∿

In the Dzogchen system, meditation and postmeditation are indivisible. There is no division between the two because the practice during the postmeditation is the meditation state itself. Mingle the view with the four daily activities of eating, lying down, walking about and sitting.

∿

In Dzogchen the word meditation means to remain in rigpa, while postmeditation means to stray into the expression of rigpa. Some people think that meditation is good, something to be adopted and that the postmeditation is bad, something to be abandoned. But that is not the case. There does not need to be a difference between meditation and postmeditation. In meditation, remain in awareness; in postmeditation, also remain in awareness. No division between sessions and breaks, rest continuously in the undivided state.

ༀ

SHAMATHA AND VIPASHYANA
ཞི་གནས་དང་ལྷག་མཐོང་།

There are two types of shamatha: 'conceptual shamatha' with involvement in concepts and 'nonconceptual shamatha' which is the practice of naturally resting in awareness. Without departing from the state of nonconceptual shamatha, engage in daily life in order to develop the strength of vipashyana.

ༀ

In fact, there is no attainment of buddhahood disconnected from shamatha and vipashyana. Though one could slightly put down their ordinary, conceptual aspects since a conceptual training is not the true cause of enlightenment.

ༀ

The extraordinary shamatha, resting in the stillness free from conceptual thinking should be combined with the extraordinary vipashyana, which is recognizing the nature of that stillness. In that way, shamatha and vipashyana are unified. This is also called the unity of awareness and emptiness.

෨

Shamatha and vipashyana are ultimately indivisible. Both are naturally included and practiced in Ati Yoga. The extraordinary shamatha is to resolve and remain in the true emptiness itself. Rather than the mere idea of emptiness, we resolve emptiness in actuality, in direct experience, and remain naturally in that state. The genuine shamatha is to not create anything artificial whatsoever, but to simply remain in the experience of emptiness. Vipashyana means not to deviate from that state.

෨

Every vehicle, beginning with the shravaka vehicle, practices shamatha and vipashyana, so do not think that these two are discarded at the level of Dzogchen. On the contrary, on the Ati level, the shamatha aspect is the innate stability in the nondual state of awareness, while the awake or cognizant quality is the vipashyana aspect. Our basic nature, also called cognizant wakefulness, is resolved through shamatha and vipashyana. Neither of these is fabricated in any way. The shamatha that is not needed is the stillness of mind-made fabrication.

❧

According to the ordinary system, one first cultivates shamatha and then pursues vipashyana. Cultivating shamatha means to produce a state of mental stillness and to train in it. Pursuing the insight of vipashyana means to try to find who the meditator is; trying to identify what it is that remains quiet. It is evident that both of these practices are involved in conceptual thinking. Only in the Essence Mahamudra and Dzogchen systems is emptiness left without fabrication. In Dzogchen, from the very first, emptiness is resolved without any need to manufacture it. Dzogchen emphasizes stripping awareness to its naked state and not clinging to emptiness in any way whatsoever. The true and authentic shamatha and vipashyana are the empty and cognizant nature of mind.

ॐ

SINGLE SPHERE OF DHARMAKAYA

ཆོས་སྐུ་ཐིག་ལེ་ཉག་གཅིག

The single sphere of dharmakaya is simply original wakefulness. It is called single or sole, meaning not a duality, whereas the normal thinking mind is dualistic and never a single unity.

ॐ

SLEEP

We have been asleep since beginningless time. Sleep is one of seven subsidiary thought states of closed-minded ignorance. It is not ignorance itself, which means being unaware or ignorant of the true nature.

Actual ignorance, like the king of stupidity, is not knowing our basic nature. Sleep is like his minister.

ॐ

We have never truly awakened from the sleepy state of primordial ignorance, but when we recognize the natural face of awareness, in a glimpse, it is as if we are just about to wake up. It is like having a light sleep in the morning, one is not completely awake yet. In fact, we are still dreaming, because apart from that glimpse of awareness, we take everything as being totally real and concrete, like a person who believes his dream experience is definitely happening.

ॐ

SPACE

ནམ་མཁའ།

All outer perceived objects are actually space that neither arises, remains nor ceases. At the same time, the nature of the perceiving mind is beyond arising, dwelling and ceasing as well. It is not some 'thing' that comes into being, remains or ceases. So, it is not only the mind that is empty while objects are real and concrete. If that were true, there could not be any mingling of space and awareness. Both the outside and the inside, both perceived objects and the perceiving subject are already beyond arising, dwelling and ceasing. Therefore, it *is* possible to train in mingling space and awareness.

ॐ

Two basic principles in the innermost Dzogchen teachings are basic space and awareness, in Tibetan *ying* and *rigpa*. Space and awareness are all-encompassing and indivisible. Space is the absence of mental constructs. Awareness means knowing that basic space is devoid of constructs, recognizing the complete emptiness of mind-essence. Our basic state is the unity of emptiness and cognizance, of space and wakefulness.

ॐ

In the basic space that is unimaginable, remain undistractedly. Let your indescribable awareness remain undistracted in the naked state of basic space. It does not have to be imagined, because this basic space that is utterly naked is our own nature already.

ॐ

STABILITY

བརྟན་པ་ཐོབ་པ།

When a child is born, it does not immediately have the power of a twenty-five year old. Slowly, slowly it will grow up. After recognition of the awakened state has taken birth, you still have to perfect the training and attain stability.

First, we must recognize our own buddha nature. Next, we must endeavor with great diligence to continuously sustain that recognition, which is called training. Finally, to reach the state where not even an iota of conceptual thinking remains, when conceptual thinking is totally purified, is called the attainment of stability. This stability is also known as the complete enlightenment of buddhahood.

Words, it is said, are like rice husks. When one has finally attained a fair bit of stability in one's practice one can acknowledge, "I have been so entangled, so involved in these words." Compared to this naked self-existing awareness words are misleading. Like rice husks, one will gradually cast away words, as one's view deepens.

ৡ

Unless this mind attains some stability in the recognition of its own natural state of original wakefulness, there will be no end to its suffering.

ৡ

Recognize, perfect the strength of that recognition, attain stability, and you are a buddha.

ৡ

SUSTAIN

We realize that this fantastic thing called buddha nature, our mind essence, is not out of reach at all. Since it is not very complex, simply allow it to be regularly sustained. When recognizing your natural face is totally effortless, you have established the natural state.

ৡ

Sustaining the natural face of mind nature does not mean to deliberately hold such a state. It means to allow its continuity without something being sustained or someone to sustain it.

ॐ

SUSTAINING FRESHNESS
སོར་གཞག

Mingling awareness with your daily activities is, in the Trekchö system also known as sustaining freshness. You try to train while engaging in daily activities without moving away from the natural state, without being distracted and without clinging. This training is to transcend the way most people meditate: keeping undistracted while still fixating.

ॐ

TERMA
གཏེར་མ།

Before Padmasambhava left Tibet, he concealed, for the benefit of future practitioners of every century — within solid rock, in lakes, even in space, an abundance of hidden terma treasures, containing teachings, precious stones and sacred articles.

෴

TERTÖNS

All great tertöns are masters who in body, speech and mind are blessed and empowered personally by Padmasambhava. Tertöns appear to reveal the hidden treasures he buried in Tibet and other countries.

෴

From childhood, a great tertön is unlike other children. He has pure visions of deities and realization overflows from within. Tertöns are not like us ordinary people who must follow the gradual path of study and practice. Ordinary people do not have instantaneous realization!

෴

When the time comes for the different terma teachings to be revealed, great tertöns appear in this world. They are able to dive into lakes, fly up to impossible locations in caves and take objects out of solid rock.

ༀ

THOUGHTFREE WAKEFULNESS

རྣམ་པར་མི་རྟོག་པའི་ཡེ་ཤེས།

Thoughtfree means free of conceptual thinking, and wakefulness means that the knowing quality is not lost.

ༀ

Yeshe, original wakefulness, implies an absence of clinging to subject and object, perceiver and perceived. This is not the case with normal mind, which is always structured as the duality of perceiver and perceived.

ༀ

You cannot relinquish one thought by grasping onto another. In the moment of recognizing the authentic thoughtfree wakefulness, every type of discursive thought movement is destroyed.

ༀ

THOUGHTS, THINKING
རྣམ་རྟོག

Thoughts are like bubbles in water; when not clung to they arise within the water and dissolve back into the water. Really, for a true yogi there is no harm no matter how wildly the thoughts move. The state without any thought movement, the indifferent state of absent-mindedness is a greater enemy.

Thought means thinking and unenlightened sentient beings think. Let go of the thoughts of the three times, not by throwing them away — that is only more thinking — but by letting go. In the moment of seeing the essence, the thoughts of the three times are automatically dissolved, disbanded.

By recognizing the empty essence in a thought, it vanishes like a bubble in water. That is how to deal with any particular thought at hand. Once you know how to let the present thought dissolve, any subsequent thought can be dealt with in exactly the same way, as simply another present thought. But if we get involved in the thought, thinking of what is being thought of and continuing it, then there is no end.

The thoughtfree state of awareness is free from dualistic clinging, free from concepts. It does not mean a state of mindless cessation.

The awakened state free from thoughts of the three times is the buddha mind.

We need to train in this nondual awareness right now. Nothing else can stop our thinking and if thinking does not stop, neither does samsara — it continues on. Samsara needs our thinking to perpetuate itself, only our own thoughts can keep it alive.

The moment you shatter the chain of thinking, you are free from the three realms of samsara.

THREEFOLD SKY

ནམ་མཁའ་སུམ་སྦྱགས།

In the context of the threefold sky practice, external space is defined as a clear sky free from the defects of clouds, mist and haze. This external sky is an example for the actual inner space and is used as a support for recognizing it. The inner space is the nature of mind, a state that is already empty. The innermost or basic space is the recognition of the unconstructed buddha nature. The innermost space is actually nondual awareness itself.

༈

Why should we engage in this threefold sky practice? Space, by itself, is totally unconfined. There is no center and no edge in any direction whatsoever. Directing the gaze into the midst of empty space is an aid for allowing the experience of the similarly unconfined and all-pervasive state of rigpa.

༈

Simply leave the state of mind that you have recognized suspended within unconfined external space. The means is the space of the external sky; the knowledge is the awareness that has been pointed out by your root guru. When suspended like this, you do not need to try to mingle space and awareness — they are already mingled.

In the ultimate sense, space and awareness are a unity. Placing unfixated awareness in supportless space serves as an enhancement for the view.

THREE BASIC PRINCIPLES
ཁྱེར་སོ་གསུམ།

All appearances are the mandala of the deities, all sounds are the mandala of mantra and all thoughts are the mandala of enlightened mind. The nature of all apparent and existing things — of this entire world and all beings within it — is the great mandala of the manifest ground, our basic state. These three mandalas are present as our ground. The practice of a sadhana is based on the principle of manifesting from this ground.

THREE EXCELLENCES

དམ་པ་གསུམ།

Never forget the excellent preparation of bodhichitta, the excellent main part beyond concepts, and the excellent conclusion of dedicating the merit.

Begin your practice with the excellent preparation of bodhichitta, including both the relative and ultimate state of awakened mind. Continue your practice with the main part of development stage and completion stage, free from concepts. Conclude your practice with dedicating the merit and making aspirations for the welfare of others. By doing so, you are combining all the teachings of Sutra and Tantra. These three excellences are, therefore, extremely important. Any practice we do while possessing the three excellences is always correct, while any practice we do while lacking them is never really perfect.

Our originally enlightened essence contains within itself the awakened state of all buddhas as the three aspects of vajra body, vajra speech and vajra mind. The training in these three vajras is complete within the profound state of samadhi, which is none other than your own nature. That is the starting point or source of the excellent main part beyond concepts.

THREE KAYAS

Even though we wander in samsara, the essence of our minds is the three kayas. We become enlightened by recognizing, training in and attaining stability in this essence.

The indivisible three kayas, our own nature is an incessant presence, not something that sometimes occurs, vanishes, and comes back.

The minds of sentient beings have the nature of the three kayas. Impurity comes about when failing to recognize what our nature really is. That temporary obscuration can again be purified.

We need to know what is, as it is. In essence, the three poisons are the three wisdoms. To be able to transform poison into medicine, we definitely need pith instructions. Through the pith instructions, the suffering of a sentient being can be transformed into wisdom. The Ati Yoga path means to possess the universal panacea that can cure all diseases. Our basic state consisting of essence, nature and capacity is the identity of the three kayas — when it is recognized!

༄

Among the two kayas, dharmakaya and rupakaya, dharmakaya is a body of space, free from constructs. Rupakaya consists of two types: the sambhogakaya, which is of rainbow light, and the nirmanakaya, which is a material body of flesh and blood possessing the six elements.

༄

Kayas and wisdoms are essential principles. It is said, "If the kayas and wisdoms are empty, there is no fruition." The dharmakaya free from constructs like space is defined as 'dissolved yet unobscured'. 'Dissolved' means totally free of all disturbing emotions. At the same time, unobscured means original wakefulness.

Dissolved yet unobscured is also called the dharmakaya of basic brilliance. Dharmakaya is not empty of the cognizant quality.

ॐ

Dharmakaya is the unity of experience and emptiness. Primordial purity is the empty aspect, while spontaneous presence is the experience aspect. These two are a unity. That is why we say that the kayas and wisdoms are a unity.

ॐ

THREE AND FIVE POISONS

དུག་གསུམ་དང་དུག་ལྔ།

Why are there sidetracks, errors and hindrances on the path? In terms of the view, it is because of the mind's dualistic clinging — passion, aggression and delusion. These three poisons are thought movements provoked by habitual patterns.

ॐ

Without exception, every thought we have is mixed with the three poisons. Just as poison causes death when ingested, the three poisonous emotions take the life of liberation when they are given free rein. We may not even notice that our minds are occupied by the three poisons producing negative karma. When the master — our mind with the three poisons — commands, his servants, our body and voice, carry out the command. In this way, we continue roaming around in samsara, continuously turning our backs on the three kayas, the very basis for all of samsara and nirvana. Instead, we create the causes for the three lower realms.

The essence of the five poisons is the five wisdoms. The methods that suppress the poisons do not reveal these wisdoms. Just like darkness cannot remain when the sun rises, none of the disturbing emotions can endure within the recognition of mind nature. That is the moment of realizing original wakefulness, and it is the same principle for each of the five poisons.

As we continue practicing, karmas and habitual patterns gradually fall apart. As they fall apart, it becomes easier to recognize and easier to maintain. That's why true yogis say, "It has become much easier and simpler for me to recognize and maintain the practice."

This is because their passion, aggression and delusion have lessened and the flawless dharmakaya is more often nakedly present.

THREE PRECEPTS
 སྡོམ་པ་གསུམ།

In the Tibetan tradition, the example for possessing the three precepts complete and without conflict is an earthen pot with milk and butter, the essence of the milk. First, the vows of the *pratimoksha*, individual liberation, are like an earthen pot. The bodhisattva trainings are likened to the milk poured into the pot. The secret samayas of Vajrayana are like the butter contained in the milk. In this way, the three sets of vows are without conflict and do no harm to one another. The vessel-like pratimoksha vows without the bodhisattva precepts are like having an empty vessel. You must have compassion, like the milk in the pot. Compassion that is not embraced by the view is like skim milk without butter, so you need the Vajrayana samadhi of cognizant emptiness.

THREE ROOTS

རྩ་བ་གསུམ།

The root of blessings is the guru, the root of the siddhis is the yidam, and the root of activities is the dakini and Dharma protectors. By practicing the three roots as your 'back support' you will not fall under the power of obstacles on the path.

THREE SAMADHIS

ཏིང་འཛིན་རྣམ་གསུམ།

The main part of a sadhana includes an aspect for body, speech and mind. The part for body involves the development stage. The mandala of the deities is visualized out of the expanse of the three kayas and unfolds out of the three samadhis. The samadhi of suchness is the intent of primordial purity, the dharmakaya. The samadhi of illumination is the intent of spontaneous presence, the sambhogakaya. The samadhi of the seed-syllable is the nirmanakaya aspect, the indivisibility of primordial purity and spontaneous presence. This is how to begin the sadhana practice.

The real way of practicing the unity of development and completion requires that you have been introduced to the view of Trekchö, cutting through, the real samadhi of suchness. The samadhi of suchness is emptiness and the samadhi of illumination is the cognizant or luminous quality. Like the example of a clean mirror, anything can be reflected. When reflected, the reflection has no materiality whatsoever and yet, it is clearly visible. The seed samadhi, the third of the three samadhis, is like the reflection appearing, while the brightness and the mirror itself are like the first two samadhis, emptiness and cognizance. These two are indivisible, and out of this indivisible unity, also called emptiness and compassion, any reflection can manifest; any form of development stage can take place freely. Without recognizing the completion stage, development stage is like the construction work going on outside my room; something is visible, but also tangible. Whatever unfolds as development stage indivisible from completion stage is experienced, but it has no material nature.

ॐ

Carry out whatever yidam practice you are involved in while practicing it within the structure of the three samadhis and while recognizing mind essence. If you practice like that, I can guarantee that within this one lifetime you can accomplish both the common siddhis and the supreme siddhi of complete enlightenment.

࿇

THREE SEATS OF COMPLETENESS

གདན་གསུམ་ཚང་བ།

Vajrayana is not a clever system of invented techniques. The nature of the peaceful and wrathful deities is present as our physical and mental make-up, as the nature of the aggregates, elements and sense-bases. These deities are also called the *three seats of completeness*. These three are the male and female tathagatas as the aggregates and elements, the male and female bodhisattvas as the sense-bases, and the male and female gatekeepers as the times and views.

࿇

THREE UNMISTAKEN QUALITIES

ཆད་མ་གསུམ།

There is the unmistaken quality of the Buddha's words, the unmistaken quality of the statements of noble beings and enlightened masters and the unmistaken quality of our root guru's oral instructions which we put into practice. By combining these unmistaken qualities with their own experience, innumerable people have been able to reach a state totally free from doubt. Moreover, they attained great accomplishments, so they could fly through the sky, pass freely through solid rock, and, without leaving a physical body behind, go to the celestial realms at the time of death.

THREE VAJRAS

རྡོ་རྗེ་གསུམ།

Our essence, nature and capacity are the dharmakaya, sambhogakaya and nirmanakaya. They are also known as the three vajras that we are supposed to achieve — the vajra body, speech and mind of all the buddhas. This real and authentic state is, in itself, empty, which is dharmakaya. Its cognizant quality is the sambhogakaya. Its unconfined unity is the nirmanakaya. This indivisible identity of the three kayas is called *svabhavikakaya*, the essence body.

Everything with concrete substance is called 'form', and all forms are the unity of appearance and emptiness: that is the vajra body. All sounds are resounding and yet empty: that is the vajra speech. When we recognize awareness, we realize that it is free from arising, dwelling and ceasing: that is the vajra mind.

TRAINING

The training is simply to remain undistracted, because it is this nondistraction that takes us all the way to complete enlightenment. Nondistraction does not mean deliberately trying to be undistracted, as we do when we replace normal thoughts with the thought, "I shouldn't be distracted." It is simply to not forget. The moment we forget — and we *do* forget — both the practice and all other things are forgotten, because our attention strays. The essential point here is not in keeping undistracted in a conceptual way. It is simply allowing the state of unconfined empty cognizance, which by itself is undistracted, to continue. That is the training.

The most essential training among all Dharma practices is to recognize and be face-to-face with the three kayas — not merely once, but to grow fully used to it. By recognizing again and again, train in simply letting habitual fixation gradually fall away.

The training in recognizing mind essence is this: short moments repeated many times. There is no other way. A short duration guarantees it is the authentic mind essence, by itself. Many times ensures we grow used to it. Attempting to keep long moments of recognition simply corrupts the natural experience with a conceptual state of mind.

You need to grow used to the natural state through training. The training is simply recognizing, not a willed act of meditating. In the moment of recognizing, it is seen. In the moment of seeing, it is free. That freedom does not necessarily last long. The fact that there is no 'thing' to be seen is clearly seen as it is. It is not hidden; it is an actuality. Short moments, but repeated many times. You need to train like that. Once you are fully trained, you do not need to think twice.

You simply need to *allow* the moment of uncontrived naturalness. Instead of meditating upon it, meaning focusing, simply allow it to naturally be. The words for training and meditating sound the same in Tibetan, so to play on that — "It is more a matter of familiarization than meditation." The more you grow familiar with mind essence and the less you deliberately meditate upon it, the easier it becomes to recognize and the simpler to sustain.

TREKCHÖ AND TÖGAL

ཁྲེགས་ཆོད་དང་ཐོད་རྒྱལ།

Trekchö is to simply acknowledge that one's innate essence is empty. Tögal is to recognize that the natural display is spontaneously present. They are not our creation; they are not produced by practice. There is no imagining of anything in either Trekchö or Tögal.

ঙ

Without cutting through with Trekchö, you can't directly cross with Tögal.

ঙ

TWO ACCUMULATIONS

ཚོགས་གཉིས།

There are two kinds of accumulations: the accumulation of merit with concepts and the nonconceptual accumulation of wisdom. The accumulation of merit with concepts includes the preliminary practices, the *ngöndro.* The nonconceptual accumulation of wisdom is the abiding in the samadhi of the natural state.

ঙ

By gathering the two accumulations we unfold the two types of supreme knowledge: the knowledge that perceives whatever exists and the knowledge that perceives the nature as it is. By unfolding the two types of supreme knowledge, we realize the two kayas, dharmakaya and rupakaya. Rupakaya means 'form body' and has two aspects: sambhogakaya, which is the form of rainbow light, and nirmanakaya, which is the physical form of flesh and blood.

ॐ

The two accumulations are a summary of the Vajrayana path.

ॐ

UNCONFINED

མ་འགགས་པ།

The unity of emptiness and cognizance has an unconfined capacity. If it were blocked, we would not be able to know anything. We would be a total blank. If cognizance and emptiness were not a unity, one of them would only occur when thinking and the other would only arise when not thinking. Conceptual thought blocks, obstructs, confines; this is how development and completion can be obstructed. However, the expression of awareness is unimpeded. If this were not so, rigpa would not have any capacity. But the dharmakaya essence of cognizant emptiness *does* have a capacity. The sambhogakaya and nirmanakaya *do* manifest.

UNITY

རང་འཇུག

Wandering in samsara is the result of failing to leave space and awareness as a unity and instead splitting them up into here and there. We have projected space as being there, while regarding awareness as being here. We split this unity of space and awareness up, fell into accepting and rejecting, hope and fear, affirming and denying, grasping at objects and fixating on the subject. That is how we ended up with the duality of samsara and nirvana — grasping the nondual as two.

It is often said, "Don't project space as being there, don't grasp awareness as being here!" This is because space and awareness are a primordial unity.

❧

The reflection in a mirror has shape, it has color, but no concrete substance to grasp. Yet, while being empty, it is still visible. The unity of being empty and apparent is like the reflection in a mirror.

❧

A person may ask you, "What is mind? How is mind? Tell me briefly." You could then say, "It is the unity of being empty and cognizant." It is complete within that sentence. Its essence is empty; its nature is cognizant. Its capacity is that these two cannot be taken apart. That is the meaning of unity — impossible to separate. That unity is the special quality of Buddhism.

❧

VAJRA

རྡོ་རྗེ།

Our body, speech and mind are conditioned and so obscure the unconditioned three kayas. The meaning of vajra is unconditioned. It is not born and it cannot be burnt by fire or washed away by water. Our body can be destroyed. When we say vajra body, vajra speech and vajra mind, we use the word 'vajra' because it means changeless, impossible to destroy or annihilate.

VAJRAYANA

རྡོ་རྗེ་ཐེག་པ།

During the present Age of Strife, it seems as though people are seldom amiable; rather, they are always trying to outdo one another. Our time owes its name to this fundamental competitiveness. But this is exactly the reason that Vajrayana is so applicable to the present era. The stronger and more forceful the disturbing emotions are, the greater the potential for recognizing our original wakefulness.

There are three different approaches to applying Vajrayana in practice: taking the ground as path, taking the path as path, and taking the fruition as path. These three approaches can be understood by using the analogy of a gardener or farmer. Taking the ground or cause as path is like tilling soil and sowing seeds. Taking the path as path is like weeding, watering, fertilizing and tending crops. Taking the fruition as path is the attitude of simply picking the ripened fruit or the fully bloomed flowers. The Dzogchen approach is to take the complete result, the state of enlightenment itself, as the path.

Vajrayana is said to be a swift path to enlightenment, simply due to unifying means and knowledge, development stage and completion stage. Vajrayana practice involves combining the visualization of a deity together with the recognition of mind essence; that is why it is a swift path.

Vajrayana training is the means to realize everything as it is, to realize that all that appears and exists is the buddha mandala. That is why we train in sadhana practice.

VIEW

ལྟ་བ།

Without the view, all teachings are only expedient, superficial instructions on behavior.

ॐ

In Dzogchen, the ultimate view is to relax into nondual awareness.

ॐ

The true view is free from viewer and viewed.

ॐ

The view is to recognize our inner simplicity. Having understood that, the meditation is to remain in naturalness without fixating on anything. Once you attain the confidence in the view, even if a hundred panditas said you should doubt it, you will be certain that there is nothing higher than it.

ॐ

In the view two should become one, and the one should become placeless, objectless.

ॐ

Resting freely, pervasive and wide open — these are the three essential points of rigpa. Resting freely means that you do not focus on something as being there. Pervasiveness means to not tie something down as being here within you. Openness means to not dwell on something in between. You could also say: do not project outwardly, do not concentrate inwardly and do not place your attention in some state in between. When not doing any of these, that is the view. That is sufficient. Do not project outwardly. Do not concentrate inwardly. Do not place your mind in between. Then there is nothing to do. You have arrived at non-doing.

๛

It is extremely important to recognize the true view. At the point of genuinely recognizing the view, there is only a single sphere, the single identity of the three kayas. The moment we recognize, nirvana is no longer something to be achieved and samsara is no longer something to be abandoned. This is how samsara and nirvana 'flow together' and are contained within a single sphere. In general terms, samsara is definitely to be abandoned and nirvana to be attained. But, in all practicality, how are we going to get rid of samsara and attain nirvana? This is where the important quote comes in, "Knowing one thing, liberates all."

VISUALIZATION

གསལ་སྣང་།

At the beginning, one visualizes the yidam deity vividly once; after that, one can rest in the nonconceptual state. When stable in awareness, the expression of rigpa will appear as the visualization. Without stability, the expression becomes too forced and the essence seems to get lost. When the essence is 'out of sight', that fault may cause visualization to increase discursive thoughts.

One should visualize the deity in vivid flashes. Otherwise when you think of the head, the bottom disappears. Simply think of the whole body from the top of the head to the bottom of the feet in its entirety.

The simplistic view of the yidam deity, the palace, the ornaments, the offering of delicious food and so on is totally interconnected with the normal habitual tendencies of mundane people. It is not that deities of rainbow light have any concepts of near and far or that being praised pleases them. It is only for one's own benefit that this is done, in order to gather the accumulations and to purify bad karma and habitual tendencies. We should clearly understand the profound intent of the Vajrayana.

WISDOM

ཡེ་ཤེས།

Wisdom (*yeshe*) means primordial knowing. It is an original wakefulness that is not dependent upon an object. We get used to primordial knowing by recognizing our essence as primordial purity.

Wisdom is primordially free from distraction. The undistracted aspect is wakefulness, which is unmistaken. If you are confused, wakefulness is gone.

YIDAM

When it comes to realizing a certain yidam, the most important points are: recognize emptiness, do the practice out of compassion for all sentient beings and be free from hope and fear. If you practice in this way, you are certain to realize the deity; there is no doubt about it.

The real practice is recognizing rigpa, and you use the yidam as the external form of the practice. Although every yidam manifests in various aspects with different qualities, in essence they are all the same — the awakened state of rigpa.

Try to see yidam practice as a gift the buddhas have given us because we have requested it. When we take refuge, we are asking for protection, to be safeguarded. The real protection lies in the teachings on how to remove the obscurations and attain realization. Yidam practice provides this true protection. Through it, we can remove what needs to be removed and realize what needs to be realized, and thereby attain accomplishment.

୬

Yidam practice can be brought into your life at any situation, at any moment. You bring this practice along whether you sit or whether you walk, whatever you are involved in. Do not think that you should stop after a set number of recitations. Continue this practice your entire life. Yidam practice is such a profound support because it contains all the aspects of Vajrayana.

୬

Yidam practice is like adding oil to the fire of practice; it blazes up even higher and hotter.

୬

YOGI

རྣལ་འབྱོར་པ།

A true yogi is a practitioner who again and again recognizes mind nature. In this way, involvement in thought automatically becomes weaker, while the gap between thoughts grows longer and longer.

᭐

A swan can separate water and milk when drinking. The yogi should be like the swan in separating the milk of original wakefulness from the water of ignorance.

᭐

The practice of a true yogi is to recognize the state free of the three poisons and continuously remain undistracted.

᭐

'Yogi' means having some degree of stability in the recognition of rigpa. For such a practitioner, everything looks different. And reality *is* different from how ordinary people believe it to be and experience it. Padmasambhava and Milarepa were not obstructed by what we believe to be solid matter. The seeming solidity of their own bodies and the seeming solidity of matter were totally interpenetrable. They could walk on water and were unharmed by fire.

᭐

A yogi is an individual who connects with that which is naturally so. Yoga means to bring the natural state into actual experience. The one who does this can truly be called a yogi. If view, meditation and conduct are mixed with concepts, such a person is not a Dzogchen yogi. Once you have recognized the natural state — in other words, once it is an actuality in your living experience — people can truly say, "The yogi has arrived," when you walk into a room! Your body is still that of a human being, but your mind is Mahamudra.

A yogi, a true practitioner, is someone who has been introduced to the natural state and is 'undivided empty cognizance suffused with knowing', the three kayas. A yogi does not find it sufficient to merely have recognized. Without training, the strength of that recognition will never be perfected and there is no stability. A yogi trains in this until perfection, until the fruition of the three kayas.

✌

Heartfelt thanks go to our Dharma friends who worked on *Vajra Speech*: the associate editor, Michael Tweed, the proofreaders Sangye Wangchen, Joanne Larson and Idan Ruebner.

✌

Index

Vajra Speech, by Tulku Urgyen Rinpoche, renowned for his extraordinary experience and realization, is a wide ranging collection of pith instructions for the Dzogchen yogi. This Tibetan master's advice reduces negative emotions and naturally enables loving kindness, compassion and wisdom to flourish.

"A swan can separate water and milk when drinking. The yogi should be like the swan in sepa rating the milk of original wakefulness from the water of ignorance."

—*Tulku Urgyen Rinpoche*

"Compared to many years studying books and going through analytical meditation, we found it more beneficial to ask questions of Tulku Urgyen and listen to his answers."

—*Orgyen Topgyal Rinpoche*

www.**rangjung**.com

Rangjung Yeshe
PUBLICATIONS
PUBLISHERS GROUP WEST

US $15.00 / $17.00 CAN
ISBN 978-962-7341-44-4

9 789627 341444   51500